LOVE
ON ITS
KNEES

John Hankerson

LOVE ON ITS KNEES

What does God want from us?

JOHN HANKERSON

Love On It's Knees by John Hankerson
Copyright © 2025 by John Hankerson
All Rights Reserved.
ISBN: 978-1-59755-843-3

Published by: ADVANTAGE BOOKS™
Orlando, FL, www.advbookstore.com

All Rights Reserved. This book and parts thereof may not be reproduced in any form, stored in a retrieval system or transmitted in any form by any means (electronic, mechanical, photocopy, recording or otherwise) without prior written permission of the author, except as provided by United States of America copyright law.

Unless otherwise noted, all scriptures are from THE HOLY BIBLE, NEW INTERNATIONAL VERSION®. Copyright© 1973, 1978, 1984, 2011 by Biblica, Inc.™. Used by permission of Zondervan

Biblical quotations marked ESV are taken from the THE HOLY BIBLE, ENGLISH STANDARD VERSION® Copyright© 2001 by Crossway, a publishing ministry of Good News Publishers. Used by permission.

Biblical quotations marked RSV are from the THE HOLY BIBLE REVISED STANDARD VERSION®, Copyright© 1952 by National Council of the Churches of Christ in the USA.

Library of Congress Catalog Number: 2025940134

Name:	**Hankerson**, John., Author
Title:	*Love On It's Knees*
	John Hankerson
	Advantage Books, 2025
Identifiers:	Paperback: 9781597558433
	eBook: 9781597558631
Subjects: Books ›	Religion: Christian Life - Inspirational

First Printing: August 2025
25 26 27 28 29 30   10 9 8 7 6 5 4 3 2 1

Table of Contents

ACKNOWLEDGMENTS 7
PREFACE 9
INTRODUCTION 13
I: THOUGHTS ON WORSHIP 17
II: LET US BOW DOWN 23

    PERSONAL, PHYSICAL EXPRESSION 25
    ACTION 29
    MUSIC 29
    IT MUST BE GOD-FOCUSED 30
    IT MUST REFLECT OUR STATUS AS CREATURES 31

III: THE SACRIFICE 37

    BROKEN RELATIONSHIPS 42

IV: THE CELEBRATION 45
V: FOREVER HIS 55
VI: MY WORSHIP 67
VII: OUR WORSHIP 79
VIII: CULTURE MATTERS 89
IX: ELEMENTS OF WORSHIP 101
X: THE ORDER OF WORSHIP 107
AFTERWORD 113

John Hankerson

Acknowledgments

Special thanks to four dear friends (Curt Flory, Lance Holemon, Terry Cooney and Mark Englizian) who agreed to read this and provide insight, commentary and occasional corrections of grammar and punctuation (which a former English teacher should not have required. As I told my student, proofread and then do it again: And much appreciation to Josh Holloran for his creative work on graphics for the book cover.

And my love and thanks to my wife Ann and our children, Carrie, Adam and Brian who have loved me and taught me much about God's love as we have lived life together.

John Hankerson

Preface

..."*there is in my heart as it were a burning fire shut up in my bones, and I am weary withholding it in, and I cannot.*" *(Jeremiah 20: 9 ESV)*

What follows is the work of a layperson, a follower of Jesus whose faith journey has been--I suspect--quite ordinary. I am not a theologian though I have studied theology. I am not a pastor though I shepherded my children daily during their childhood and often wonder how different the two roles are. I am not a musician though I can bang out a tune or two on the piano. I've often been caught singing in the shower on occasion, and I have not stood before a congregation on Sunday morning to "lead worship" though I regularly gather with other believers to worship. I will interject here with a comment made by my son Adam as he read this book: "Dad, you do have the credentials to write this book!" He reminded me that I do have a master's in theology from Fuller Seminary, an MBA from Stanford University and a master's in education also from Stanford also a 50-year walk with Jesus. He said, "Don't try to talk me out of reading the book in the introduction!" I had to laugh but I do understand his insight and wisdom and his love for me, so Adam...Thank you."

I do want to learn to love and follow and worship my Lord more fully with each passing day. I do believe that we have, for too long, been content to continue what was done in the past with no thought about its relevance or applicability. God has un-searchable blessings in store for us. He "has also set eternity in the hearts of" his creation (Ecclesiastes 3:11), an eternity that He designed for us to experience in the here and now. Jesus regularly reminded the disciples the kingdom of God was here and now also in the future. To realize that kingdom here is, I believe, deeply entangled with our worship. I hope to collect what God has said about these blessings in the text that follows.

If pastors and theologians read these pages, they will possibly uncover several theological challenges to these ideas. For the most part, I have relied only on Scripture and my knowledge of church history. Where I could, I have examined the linguistic roots of certain words using tools easily handled by the layman. And I have drawn on my and others' experiences of worship in the modern church.

Finally, I have chosen to begin with a "blank slate." I start with no preconceived ideas about what worship is or what it should look like. The fact the church has done certain things in the past is of interest to me ultimately, but in developing a biblical idea of worship, I start with Scripture alone. We can and should learn from history but when history and not Scripture becomes normative, I usually find myself running the other way.

My read on the 4th chapter of the Book of Revelation is that eternity we will spend in "living worship." If that is so, what better way to prepare than to begin learning now what worship can and should be.

The title may inspire more discussion given the events in recent years in the United States with NFL players kneeling for the National Anthem rather than standing in respect. What I find most interestingly absent from this discussion is what it means when we kneel. In this case, the players ascribed a certain meaning to their action but that meaning does not appear linked to what kneeling meant in western culture in the past. Instead, I find a "new meaning" being ascribed to kneeling, a meaning set against the meaning given to "standing" for the anthem. The ease with which we transfer and/or give alternative meanings to actions ought to give us pause as we discuss what worship is, what it should be, and what it means to us.

John Hankerson

Introduction

When they were growing up, my kids regularly asked, "Are we going to church tomorrow? Can't we just go to Sunday school?" The good news here was they liked Sunday school; the bad news was the Sunday service had no appeal. "It's too long" and "It's boring" were the two most common explanations. On one typical Sunday, my daughter burst into tears at the thought that we would be going to both the "worship service" and Sunday school. At the same time my son reminded me that "there is nothing to do" in the worship service. As a father, I am unsettled by this response. I suppose I feel responsible that my kids don't want to go to church and somewhere in my Christian experience, I have been told they should. The fact of the matter is though, that all too often, I don't find myself attracted to "church" on Sunday mornings either. Shouldn't going to church be as Richard Foster describes it:

> *"To worship is to experience Reality, to touch life. It is to know, to feel, to experience the resurrected Christ amid the gathered community. It is a breaking into the Shekinah of God, or better yet, being invaded by the Shekinah of God." (Celebration of Discipline, p. 158)*

I don't know about you but that sounds exciting and attractive to me. If that is what "church" was like, I bet my kids, and your kids, would want to go more often than just on Sunday. You and I would find the Sunday morning event more than an obligation or duty, more than a responsibility, and more than a weekly fellowship or learning opportunity. It would become a joyful, shared, energizing encounter with the living God, the God who makes us a community, not just a collection of individuals who happen to share a creed.

So why do we go to "church" on Sunday mornings? Rick Warren identifies at least one reason people do NOT go to church on Sunday in his book, *The Purpose Driven Church*. Here he lists one common complaint about churches in his area, that "church is boring, especially the sermons; the messages don't relate to my life." Some believers expect a stimulating experience and an interesting sermon from the Sunday morning event.

I recently led a group of adults looking at what worship meant biblically. At the first class, I asked the group why they came to "Sunday Service." You should note I did not call it "worship" because I didn't want to assume that what the church does on Sunday morning is worship. I merely wanted to start with a look at what believers expect Sunday morning to be about. Their answers probably will not surprise you since I suspect that most of us would give the same answers to this question.

When asked the reason for attending Sunday morning service, my group gave the following answers:

- to hear the Word of God and to learn more about Him
- to experience fellowship and community
- to grow spiritually
- to worship: praise, contemplate, pray

What I wanted to explore with this group and hope to do in this book is take these reasons…expressions of our expectations for Sunday service and examine them considering what Scripture teaches us about worship. Are these expectations consistent with what worship should be? Do we even understand what worship is and arrive

Sunday expecting to worship our God? I think much of worship in the modern evangelical church is from forms and practices of the last 150 years, practices that may no longer serve the true meaning of worship. Their roots may be in historical applications of biblical truth about worship. Although, I see little evidence that pastors or theologians have invested much effort or study in regenerating the practice of worship in the 21st century. (Remember my comment about the changing nature of the meaning of actions we are seeing in modern days!)

My premise is that the Bible does provide us with a clear definition of the nature and intent of worship but NOT the "order" or elements of worship. Those things we do, the order and content of worship, must continually be reinvented as our expressions, our symbols and our language and culture change. Worship is an expression of inner realities and our expression of those inner realities should align with our current way of looking at the world, culture, and way of being. Therefore, the order of worship cannot be constrained to an unchanging series of activities or expressions. The Roman Catholic church has struggled to adapt the Mass to modern times. Some examples: removing Latin as the language of worship, introducing different forms of music, and "folk masses" during the seventies. Yet still the problem remains the Church is bound to a tradition and a structure that does not allow for radical change. The elements of the mass (its structure) are basically fixed, leaving little room for translating the essence of the mass into our modern world. Just as a kiss or a handshake communicates different things in different cultures, the expressions of our worship must be alive and flow from the time and place where we live. In other words, our worship must be genuine, not a ritual or practice we engage in without thinking but rather a true expression of ourselves. That authentic self is much a part of our culture and time and its "flavor" should be reflected in our worship. We respond to God's grace and love in ways that are authentic, not forced or mindless ritual but REAL. Chapter VII will explore some of these ideas in greater detail.

The purpose of this book is to develop a biblical understanding of worship and then to consider how this model might be applied to individual, family and community expressions of worship today. My prayer is that we can begin to know what it will be like to experience His presence more fully through our worship.

I

Thoughts On Worship
Spiritual Leaders Weigh In

Before I dig into my thoughts on worship, I thought it might be helpful to include several of my favorite descriptions of worship from pastors, theologians, evangelists and other laypersons like me. My hope is that as you sit with each of these descriptions and comments, you will be moved to consider that perhaps our view of worship has been too small for too long.

> *"When we think about the greatness, the glory, and the wonder of God, what do we want? True worship is the desire to merge with God, for him to possess us and us to possess him. That is what Jesus says happens when we eat and drink his life. When we come and believe in him, and keep coming and keep believing in him, we grow into an intimate relationship with God.*
>
> *"Jesus has modeled this for us: 'As the living Father sent me, and I live by means of the Father [this was the secret of his life], so he who eats me will live by means of me. That is a wonderful description of the Christian life. Jesus lived by means of the Father, and we are to live by means of him in everything we do.'*
>
> *You in me, and I in you. That is what I want to experience more of, Lord. Help me to keep coming to you and to keep trusting in you to provide all that I need."* --Ray Stedman

" 'Worship' is the term we use to cover all the acts of the heart and mind and body that intentionally express the infinite worth of God...Worship is basically adoration." --John Piper

"I can safely say, on the authority of all that is revealed in God's Word, that any man or woman who is bored and turned off by worship is not ready for heaven." -- A.W. Tozer

"I need to worship because without it I can forget that I have a big God beside me and live in fear. I need to worship because without it I can forget his calling and begin to live in a spirit of self-preoccupation. I need to worship because without it I lose a sense of wonder and gratitude and plod through life with blinders on. I need to worship because my natural tendency is toward self-reliance and stubborn independence." -- John Ortberg

"You never go away from us, yet we have difficulty in returning to You. Come, Lord, stir us up and call us back. Kindle and seize us. Be our fire and our sweetness. Let us love. Let us run." -- Augustine of Hippo

"Nothing teaches us about the preciousness of the Creator as much as when we learn the emptiness of everything else." -- Charles Spurgeon

"Many Spirit-filled authors have exhausted the thesaurus to describe God with the glory He deserves. His perfect holiness, by definition, assures us that our words can't contain Him. Isn't it a comfort to worship a God we cannot exaggerate?" -- Francis Chan

Worship is the proper response of all moral, sentient beings to God, ascribing all honor and worth to their Creator-God

1: THOUGHTS ON WORSHIP – Spiritual Leaders Weigh In

precisely because he is worthy, delightfully so." -- D.A. Carson

"Worship has been misunderstood as something that arises from a feeling which 'comes upon you. But it is vital that we understand that it is rooted in a conscious act of the will, to serve and obey the Lord Jesus Christ." -- Graham Kendrick

"The worship to which we are called in our renewed state is far too important to be left to personal preferences, to whims, or to marketing strategies. It is the pleasing of God that is at the heart of worship. Therefore, our worship must be informed at every point by the Word of God as we seek God's own instructions for worship that is pleasing to Him." -- R.C. Sproul

"Put it this way: if your idea of God, if your idea of the salvation offered in Christ, is vague or remote, your idea of worship will be fuzzy and ill-formed. The closer you get to the truth, the clearer beauty becomes, and the more you will find worship welling within you. That's why theology and worship belong together. The one isn't just a head trip; the other isn't just emotion." -- N.T. Wright

"We should know and celebrate God with our whole person. While too many Christians neglect to serve God with the mind, others cultivate only their minds and neglect the emotional aspects of worship." -- Craig S. Keener

"Work becomes worship when you dedicate it to God and perform it with an awareness of his presence." -- Rick Warren

"Cause every task of your day to be a sacred ministry to the Lord. However mundane your duties, for you they are a sacrament." -- Richard Foster

"But just as your body needs sleep, your soul needs time to rest in God. To learn more about Him. To talk to Him. To worship and praise Him. To fellowship with other brothers and sisters." -- Craig Groeschel

"From your heroes you pick up mannerisms and phrases and tones of voice and facial expressions and habits and demeanors and convictions and beliefs. The more admirable the hero is and the more intense your admiration is, the more profound your transformation will be. In the case of Jesus, he is infinitely admirable, and our admiration rises to the most absolute worship. Therefore, when we behold him as we should, the change is profound." -- John Piper

"The highest form of worship is the worship of unselfish Christian service." -- Billy Graham

"God directs his people not simply to worship but to sing his praises 'before the nations.' We are called not simply to communicate the gospel to nonbelievers; we must also intentionally celebrate the gospel before them." -- Timothy J. Keller

WOW! I am deeply humbled by these great insights and comments. I do not know about you, but I am awestruck by what these devout believers have to say about our God and our worship of Him. I am also feeling a wee bit inadequate to tackle a subject so complex and so important as worship but tackle it I will. I hope these comments and what follows will motivate you to bow down to the God who

1: THOUGHTS ON WORSHIP – Spiritual Leaders Weigh In

made you and who loves you. A God who wants to be in an intimate relationship with you every minute of every day.

John Hankerson

II

Let Us Bow Down

"There is no narrowing so deadly as the narrowing of man's horizon of spiritual things. No worse evil could befall him in his course on earth than to lose sight of heaven." (Inscription outside Stanford Memorial Church)

Before tackling what the Old Testament says about worship and what it meant to the Jewish community, I want to share a comment from one of Ray Stedman's sermons. He said, "...*human folly takes many forms: either self-sufficiency—man imagining he is God, and he can run the world—or idolatry, where man trusts something else as god other than the true God.*" Worship requires a clear understanding of who we are (not sufficient) and who God is (the One whom we need and from whom our sufficiency comes). Our self-knowledge must reveal that we desperately need Him, and I believe it is out of that deep need and recognition of what that means for our relationship with Him that our worship arises. John Calvin comments on this very thing when he writes:

On the other hand, it is evident man never attains to a true self-knowledge. Until he has previously contemplated the face of God and come down after such contemplation to look into himself. For (such is our innate pride) we always seem to ourselves just, upright, wise and holy, until we're convinced, by clear evidence, of our injustice, vileness, folly, and impurity. Convinced, however, we are not, if we look to ourselves only, and not to the Lord also – He, being the only standard by the application of which this conviction can be produced. For, since we are all naturally prone to hypocrisy, any empty likeness of righteousness is enough to satisfy us instead of righteousness itself. (Institutes Book 1 Chapter 1)

I believe we will find the Old Testament affirms these ideas: that we need God, that we are not sufficient in ourselves, and that worship is a response to these truths.

I am struck by how rarely we look to Old Testament Scripture to understand what worship is. Perhaps because most of us believe the worship of the Old Testament was so ritualistic, so choreographed, that it has little if anything to say to us today. Perhaps because the New Testament church either worshipped in synagogues (which sounds like the Old Covenant) or gathered in homes (with their limited capacity unlike today's mega churches, let alone small, couple-of-hundred member congregations). If we are to understand the meaning and purpose of worship, I believe we must understand it in the full sweep of Scripture beginning with the Old Testament.

I know a little Old Testament Hebrew and can find my way around a concordance. So, I want to examine the words the Old Testament Scripture uses for worship and consider their relevance for us today. There are two Hebrew words most often translated "worship" in English: "shachah" and "cegid."[1] These words appear some 100 times in various forms. Both words mean essentially the same thing in English: to prostrate, to bow down the self, to crouch or fall flat, to humbly beseech, to do reverence. Those of us who are not history buffs (or remember high school social studies as disinteresting) might want to take a walk back in time to the days when kings ruled much of the world. Respect shown to kings has a lot in common with the Hebrew words for worship. Kings and monarchs throughout history received honor and respect in various forms. But most prominent has always been some physical expression of humility: curtsies, bows, kneeling before the king, entering the presence of the king on one's knees, even laying oneself at the feet of the king. This reverence or homage is not always reserved for royalty as we see even in modern cultures where it is a sign of respect to bow to one's elders or even to one's peers. This personal, physical expression with our bodies is the first element I would like to consider, followed by two more: acts of worship, and music in worship.

Personal, Physical Expression

Physical acts, like many other things in life, take on symbolic or representational significance. What does kneeling before another symbolize? By prostrating ourselves in the presence of another, what are we communicating? If you are like most Americans in the 21st century, the thought of bowing down before anyone or anything is as foreign as washing the feet of guests who come to our home. We pride ourselves on our self-reliance, our individual ability and worth, our independence. We don't like to admit even in the quiet of our prayer time that we have needs, that we might not be up to a task, or that we have failed. It's a whole lot easier for us to verbally acknowledge God is great, that we are inadequate, or that we are sinners than it is for us to show those realities for everyone to see. What does the physical act of bowing down mean or symbolize? At its heart, bowing down is an acknowledgment that we are in the presence of one greater than ourselves. It is both a statement about the one to whom we bow, and about our own selves. When the Israelites of the Old Testament bowed down before the Ark of the Covenant, they were recognizing the holiness and the otherness of Yahweh. They were admitting their sin—their "un-holiness"—and they were admitting the authority of Yahweh over their lives. He is King.

The physical expression of reverence before the almighty Creator of the universe, kneeling and bowing and physically affirming His kingship, was not a theological act for the people of Israel. It was simply a physical expression of their position or standing in the presence of God. It showed their understanding of two things: who they are and who He is; also, their need and His provision; their unworthiness and His worthiness; their brokenness and His healing; their nature as the created and His as the Creator; their sin and His redemption; furthermore, their weakness and His greatness; altogether pointing to His worthiness to receive adoration and praise and thanksgiving.

I am reminded of a sermon given by Ray Stedman (a *profoundly influential* man in my life) where he pointed out a simple but *profound* truth in the story of Moses before the burning bush. Moses told God he was not a brave man and God answered, "I am." Moses responded that he was not a powerful speaker and God answered, "I am." Moses realized that only by relying on "The Great I Am" could these things ever come to be. By his act of accepting his weakness, he bowed down before his Creator. One of my favorite authors, C.S. Lewis, describes our sin nature as wanting to be "nouns" which stand alone in a sentence. When the reality is that we were created to be "adjectives" which only exist in connection to a noun—in this case—God. (My first career as an English teacher makes this analogy by Lewis special. Parts of speech were my thing for many years teaching writing and critical thinking. By nature, we are creatures created to "bow down" to that which is beyond us and above us. For He came to us in the person of Jesus to save us from our brokenness and separation from Him whom we were made to worship.

We westerners find it difficult to let our bodies speak for us when it comes to our faith. It is easy to leap to our feet cheering as our team

2: LET US BOW DOWN

scores the winning points. It's easy to shout out with joy as our child rounds the track at the head of the pack. But when it comes to acknowledging God's "god-ness" and our sinfulness in front of others, we tighten like a bowstring. Much is written by other writers about the difference between the Greek way of thinking about life- -the reliance on reason - more typical of the way most of us live our lives. And the Hebrew way of thinking about life--more oriented towards the doing. Suffice it to say that it is possible that we might need to work a little harder to bring our minds and our actions together in our expressions of worship. We need to learn both to "reason together" as we are called to in Isaiah 1:18 and to "Worship and bow down. To kneel before the Lord our God, our Maker." (Ps. 95:6)

Consider Jesus' final moments with the disciples at Gethsemane. Matthew describes the events with these words: "Going a little farther, he fell on his face to the ground and prayed, 'My Father, if it is possible, may this cup be taken from me. Yet not as I will, but as you will.'" Jesus himself "bows down" physically before the Father in worship, in humility, in prayer. Can we do any less? There is a kind of true humility that must lie at the heart of our worship, humility that expresses itself in physical acts of worship. Just consider a few Old Testament illustrations to bring this point home:

*"And when they heard of the Lord's concern about them and had seen their misery, they **bowed down and worshipped**." Ex. 4:31.*

*"It is the Passover sacrifice to the Lord, who passed over the houses of the Israelites in Egypt and spared our homes when he struck down the Egyptians. Then the people **bowed down and worshiped**." Ex. 12:27.*

*Joshua "fell **facedown to the ground in reverence**, and asked him, 'What message does my Lord have for his servant?'" Jos. 5:14*

*"Then David said to the whole assembly, 'Praise the Lord your God.' So, they all praised the Lord, the God of their fathers; they **bowed low and fell prostrate** before the Lord and the king." I Chron. 29:20*

*"At this Job got up and tore his robe and shaved his head. Then he **fell to the ground** in worship…" Job 1:20*

*"Let us go to his dwelling place; let us worship **at his footstool**" Ps. 132:7*

*"…they hire a goldsmith to make it into a god, and they **bow down and worship** it." Is. 46:6*

*"…you must **fall down and worship** the image of gold that King Nebuchadnezzar has set up." Dan. 3:5*

*"If you are ready to **fall down and worship** the image I made, very good." Dan. 3:15.*

Notice that there's no way the King could know whether the people were worshipping the image except for their act of **bowing down in worship.**

Worship involves a physical response; it is in many ways a call to action, a call to express our response to God who is both creator and redeemer and who is also Holy.

Action

The temple sacrifices were another physical demonstration of worship, a tangible act of God's people, an affirmation of another spiritual truth. Moses tells the people of Israel, "Take from among you an offering to the Lord" (Exodus 35:5). Their physical acts of sacrifice were statements that their sins needed to be atoned for. And that ultimately that their sins were "covered" by the blood of the sacrifice first and foremost. They also affirmed God's ownership of all creation and His provision for His people. Look at the offering described in 1 Chronicles 29:14-21 ESV: a thousand each out of the livelihood of the people. Why? Because those bulls and rams and sheep were God's to begin with.

> *"But who am I, and what is my people, that we should be able thus to offer willingly? For all things come from you, and of your own have we given you'...Bless the Lord your God." And all the assembly blessed the Lord, the God of their fathers, and **bowed their heads, and worshiped** the Lord, and did **obeisance to the King**. And they performed sacrifices to the Lord. And on the next day offered burnt offerings to the Lord, a thousand bulls, a thousand rams, and a thousand lambs, with their drink offerings, and sacrifices in abundance for all Israel. And they ate and drank before the Lord on that day, with great gladness.*

Music

Music is another element often included in Old Testament references to worship. The Psalms are our best example of the prominence of a musical response to God, but the Scriptures are filled with "songs" of God's people: Moses' song in Deuteronomy 32, Deborah's song in Judges 5, Israel's song in the wilderness in Numbers 21:17. What did the music affirm and why was it part of the community event of worship? At the least it proclaims God's kingship over the earth. It shouts His praise for the incredible work of His hands; and it expresses the joy of His people that they are called by His name and not by the names of false gods. It is not surprising to me that music has been a central element in the Church's worship life. Because music plays such a prominent role in worship throughout church history, I will devote a later chapter to a deeper examination to understand its place in our worship today.

We see that Old Testament Scripture talks about worship as an expression of the "otherness" and greatness of God, a perspective that should make a difference in our thinking about worship. From these Scriptures I conclude that our worship foremost must possess two characteristics:

It Must Be God-focused

The principal object of gathering on Sunday must be to direct our attention to our God. To acknowledge His greatness, His bounty, His unending love, and His faithfulness; and to be reminded as a body who He is in our lives. When I asked a group of adults in a Sunday school class to complete the sentence: "Worship is_____, their answers affirmed that worship must be God-focused in four significant ways.

First, our worship must focus on God by accepting Him. We acknowledge God when we affirm who He is, when we remember what He has done and is doing, when we confess His holiness; and when we declare His place in our lives. One way we do this is by physical expression. Of course, there are other ways we encounter and respond to God. Such as quiet times of reflection, times of personal prayer, meditation or simply letting our hearts rest in His presence. These are vital to our being in relationship with the One who loves us and wants to walk with us. And perhaps most importantly of all, we find Him in the pages of Scripture, discovering who He is through His revelation of Himself to us in Scripture. There we discover His heart, His will, and His love for us. Being in the Word is essential for us as individuals but also for us as a community of faith. It is primarily that community of faith and its expression of worship with which I am most concerned.

Second, worship is focused on God when He is the audience; when our words, our songs, and our prayers seek Him out. And when we come before Him with the goal of casting our praises to Him, not with a goal of getting something for ourselves. We do this through acts of worship and songs of praise and thanksgiving.

Third, worship is focused on God when it is the response of an obedient heart. We worship because we are called to worship. Worship is our "spiritual service" to God. We are called to do this in all aspects of living our lives each day.

Finally, worship is focused on God when it is a heartfelt expression of praise and adoration to our Lord.

It Must Reflect our Status as Creatures

Linked repeatedly in the Old Testament are sacrifice and worship. Sacrifice that affirmed the sin and need of the Israelites, sacrifice that affirmed the Lord's ownership over all creation and good gifts given to His people, and sacrifice that confirmed His call to obedience. Aaron received specific instructions to govern how he entered the sanctuary area of the temple, instructions that again affirm these key ideas. He was to bring a young bull as a sin offering, to make up for his failings and sins. He was to bring a ram for a burnt offering to acknowledge God's claim over all creation.

And he was to dress in sacred garments and bathe beforehand to remind himself that his God is a holy God. (Lev. 16: 3-5).

Our "creature hood" thankfully does NOT deny a central teaching of Jesus that the Father loves his people and desires to be in fellowship with them. We, the people of Israel, are called to celebrate in fellowship (Deuteronomy 27:6):

> *Build the altar of the Lord your God with fieldstones and offer burnt offerings on it to the Lord your God. Sacrifice fellowship offerings there, eating them and rejoicing in the presence of the Lord your God.*

We can and should rejoice in our worship because our God has rescued us from our sin and is in the process of building in each one of us the mind of Christ. Our worship and our fellowship both must be characterized by an **acknowledgment of our need for His power and presence, our need for one another, and the joy of being in God's presence.**

The Old Testament is rich in worship tradition but only if we have eyes to see beyond the form and into the meaning and substance of those forms. Altars, sacrifices, blood, ritual clothing are means to an end, the end being a deep awareness of God's "god-ness" and our "creatureliness." And if that is the case, what the church today must be about is finding the forms that affirm God for who He has revealed Himself to be through Scriptures. That is the task of the worshipping church, the charge of the pastor and worship leader. Our response to who God is then becomes our worship, worship that must flow out of a right understanding of who He is and who we are. I think Psalm 95 best sums up what I believe the Old Testament teaches about worship. We would do well if we could put this Psalm into our Sunday morning gathering.

2: LET US BOW DOWN

Come, let us sing for joy to the Lord; let us shout aloud to the Rock of our salvation.

Let us come before Him with thanksgiving and extoll Him with music and song.

For the Lord is the great God, the great King above all gods.

In His hands are the depths of the earth, and the mountain peaks belong to Him.

The sea is His, for He made it, and His hands formed the dry land.

Come, <u>let us bow down in worship, let us kneel before the Lord our Maker</u>. For He is our God, and we are the people of His pasture, the flock under His care.

Today, if you hear His voice, do not harden your hearts as you did at Meribah, as you did that day at Massah in the desert,

when your fathers tested and tried me, though they had seen what I did.

For forty years I was angry with that generation; I said, "They are a people whose hearts go astray, and they have not known my ways."

So, I declared on oath in my anger, "They shall never enter my rest."

The key elements are all present in this Psalm:

- We are joyful because He has saved us
- We are thankful because of His provision and His salvation
- We recognize that God is great beyond our imagining
- We acknowledge that all creation is His
- We can rest, knowing we are in His care and depend on Him in all things

One final look at an interesting verse from Judges 7:13-15:

> *Gideon arrived just as a man was telling a friend his dream. "I had a dream," he was saying. "A round loaf of barley bread came tumbling into the Midianite camp. It struck the tent with such force the tent overturned and collapsed." His friend responded, "This can be nothing other than the sword of Gideon son of Joash, the Israelite. God has given the Midianites and the whole camp into his hands." When Gideon heard the dream and its interpretation, he worshipped God. He returned to the camp of Israel and called out, "Get up! The Lord has given the Midianite camp into your hands.*

Gideon's first response is to "worship," to "shachah." He fell on his knees in joy, in thanksgiving, in awareness of God's greatness, in awe of his role in creation and secure in the knowledge that his God would deliver him. I find it amazing that his first thought is to "bow down" before his maker. His second thought is to step out in response, to express in action his love, trust and knowledge that God will bring these things about, not Gideon himself. In so many ways, Gideon was incredible—a warrior for God Himself—but even more, a man who got worship right! A man who long before Christ's coming and the gift of the Holy Spirit understood the "deep magic" as C.S. Lewis describes it-who God is and who Gideon was in relation to his Creator. He knew that he lived in complete dependence on His God for all things and out of that deep knowledge came worship.

Gideon, I believe, understood what it meant to "fear the Lord," to be in right relationship with his God. He lived out the words of Proverbs 2:1-5:

My son, if you accept my words and store up my commands within you. If you turn your ear to wisdom and apply your heart to understanding. If you call out for insight and cry aloud for understanding. And if you look for it as for silver and search for it as for hidden treasure, then you will understand the FEAR OF THE LORD and find the knowledge of God.

Gideon accepted God's words to him, stored up His commands and applied himself to hearing and understanding his Creator and acting in obedience. His life reflected the beginning of wisdom--the fear of the Lord--and produced in him a deep knowledge of and love for His (and our) God. His "fear" was a deep reverence towards God that arose out of his understanding that God was the source of his life, his strength and the things he was able to accomplish. In other words, his fear/reverence flowed out of his recognition that God was God and Gideon was His creation.

[1.] The following passages contain some form of the Hebrew word "shachah: Gen. 22:5, 24:26,28,52; Ex. 4:31, 12:27, 24:1, 32:8, 33:10, 34:8,14; De. 4:19, 11:16, 17:3, 26:10, 29:26, 30:17; Jg. 7:15; Jos. 5:14; 1Sa. 1:3,19,28, 15:25,30,31; 2Sa. 12:20, 15:32; 1Ki. 9:6,9, 11:33, 12:30, 16:31, 22:53; 2Ki. 5:18, 17:16,36, 18:22, 21:3,21; 1Ch. 16:29, 29:20; 2Ch. 7:3,19,22, 29:28,29,30, 33:3; Ne. 8:6, 9:3; Job 1:20; Ps. 5:7, 22:27, 22:29, 29:2, 45:11, 66:4, 81:9, 86:9, 95:6, 96:9, 97:7, 99:5, 99:9, 106:19, 132:7; 138:2, Isa. 2:8, 2:20, 27:13, 36:7, 46:6, 49:7, 66:23; Jer. 1:16, 7:2, 8:2, 13:10, 16:11, 22:9, 25:6, 26:2; Eze. 46:2,3,9, 8:16; Mic 5:13; Zep. 1:5,

2:11; Zec. 14:16,17. The following passages use the Hebrew word "cigid": Dan. 2:46, 3:5,7,10,12,14,15,18,28.

III

The Sacrifice

"And what does the Lord require of you? To act justly and to love mercy and to walk humbly with your God." (Micah 6:8)

Before we consider what the New Testament has to say about worship there is an important aspect to worship in the Old Testament that we have not considered. The link among words, thoughts and deeds. Words, thoughts and deeds in Hebrew history have always enjoyed the most profound marriage. Belief and action, thoughts and the doing of those thoughts were so intimately joined as to be nearly indistinguishable. Consequently, we must be careful not to overlook that for the Hebrew people, worship was a way of life as much as it was a gathering before the temple for ritual forms of worship.

The prophet Micah asks a serious question: "With what shall I come before the Lord and bow down (worship) before the exalted God?" (Micah 6:6) When we come into the presence of God, what do we have to offer to Him? What will show our humility, our acknowledgment of His greatness and our need, what will reveal our unworthiness and His worthiness, with what will we display our "worship"?

Like Micah's people, our first response might be that we will bring to Him our admission of sin, the sacrifices of a guilt offering: "Shall I come before him with burnt offerings, with calves a year old?" (6:6b) This question is the first in a series of three the prophet asks; none of the three receives a direct answer. Instead, Micah tells the people they already know the answer, they know what God expects of them in verse 8: "to act justly and to love mercy and to walk humbly with your God." Why does he not make it clear after each question that God is not really interested in the sacrifices and other ritual forms of worship but rather in a life lived in obedience? Because God cares about our acts of worship AND the acts in our lives; it is not a question of either-or but a question of both-and. Both the worshipping church and the working church are God's design. Just as prayer is both an activity/response lived in humble reliance on God; just as faith is both a belief/response to God and a lifestyle (faith without works is dead). So also, is worship both a response to God and a life lived in response to God. Our lives, when lived in dependence on God, are a continual prayer to Him, an expression of worship to Him, and a revelation of the reality of our faith in Him. We cannot and should not separate religious forms from a "religious" life. That was the mistake of the Pharisees and the recurring error of the people of Israel throughout their faith history. Life for us western Christians often makes it difficult to see our need for God. We have ready-made food, wealth that provides most of what we need and want without relying on God to provide. We have various forms of success from our efforts. It is easy to believe that our success comes from our own strength and abilities. We hardly need God until things fall apart in our lives, and we become aware that we are not in control. Then we run towards Him crying out for His help and guidance when every breath we take and every move we make is possible because He sustains us and the universe in which we live. It is hard to see our need for God in our busy lives unless we intentionally expose ourselves to God's word which will, as Calvin reminds us, bring our sin and weakness to the forefront. The Jewish people's acts of worship were constant reminders they needed Him in every aspect of their lives.

3: THE SACRIFICE

That Micah does not answer his own question directly is evidence of the nature or intention of the religious forms. The problem is the people of Israel fail to live their lives in continual reliance on their God, they fail to do justice and mercy and to walk with humility.

The prophet Isaiah takes Micah's ideas to a higher level when he rebukes the people of Israel for their inability to live a life worthy of God's call. Though the people still attend to matters of worship-- "multitude of sacrifices, burnt offerings of rams..." (Isaiah 1:11) -- they have neglected to live as God has called them to live: "your hands are full of blood." (Is. 1:15). Later, Isaiah scolds the people who have chosen to fast as a form of worship by pointing out to them that their fast is not consistent with the rest of their faith. They fast while ignoring the needs of those around them; they fast not out of love but out of duty; they fast while seeking their own pleasures:

> "Behold in the day of your fast you seek your own pleasure and oppress all your workers.
>
> Behold you fast only to quarrel and to fight and to hit with wicked fist." (Is. 58:3-4 ESV).

The worship God wants from His people is that we will be His hands on earth:

> "Is not this the fast that I choose: to loose the bonds of wickedness, to undo the thongs of the yoke, to let the oppressed go free, and to break every yoke? Is it not to share your bread with the hungry, and bring the homeless poor into your house; when you see the naked, to cover him, and not to hide yourself from your own flesh?" (Is. 58:6-7 ESV)

Micah's second question of the people is: "Will the Lord be pleased with thousands of rams, with ten thousand rivers of oil?" (Mic. 6:7) The reference to rams is understandable (life sacrificed for sin), but what is the reference to oil about? Oil was an important element in the religious ceremonies of the people of Israel. Most notably it appears to be present in the first-fruit offerings and tithing of the people. Oil was used in food preparation, in lamps to generate light, and in the consecration/dedication of kings and priests. Isaiah tells us that oil was associated with gladness (Is. 61:3) while in other references it appears to indicate things like success, spiritual sustenance, and comfort. In any case, oil was important to the people of Israel, as was their livestock (rams). Both oil and rams are important to the lives of the people. So, offering them would in fact constitute a sacrifice by the people, a giving up of something that was of great value to them. But I think Micah is pointing out another truth: the size of the offering might matter, thousands of rams, ten thousand rivers of oil, not a small sum. The act of offering such wealth to God arises out of a heart that acknowledges His claim to all we have and are. If our hearts do accept that this bounty comes from Him and that we are willing to return it to Him, should He not be pleased with our offering? I would think so, wouldn't you? But for Micah's people, it appears, though they made the offering, their hearts were elsewhere. Apparently, they were unwilling to live lives which were consistent with a belief that all they possessed came from God; they were unwilling to share with their neighbors who had need.

The third question--"Shall I offer my firstborn for my transgression, the fruit of my body for the sin of my soul?" (6:7b) --reminds us of the father of faith, Abraham. For Abraham, the sacrifice took on even deeper meaning as he realized the sacrifice also risked the promise he had received from God: namely that he would be the father of many nations. Isaac was his miracle child and the

3: THE SACRIFICE

fulfillment of God's promise. His sacrifice meant not only his obedience to God but his willingness to trust God beyond all trusting. To put all of himself, his life and future and even promises made to him, to put all of that before God in total trust. For us, the answer to Micah's question must be "yes." All we have must be available to Him as He calls. We must not only be willing to offer it all to Him but offer it all to Him: **we must live lives that reflect our having given it all to Him, all of it.**

"He has showed you, O man, what is good. And what does the Lord require of you? To act justly and to love mercy and to walk humbly with your God." (6:8)

Micah tells us that God desires that we live "just" lives, that we treat others fairly. He also tells us to "love mercy," to balance fairness/justice with mercy much as God Himself has done in Jesus for us. Finally, he calls us to "walk humbly with our God." Be fair and just, be merciful and be humble. Humility requires us to once again recognize that we desperately need to see our own weakness, our own need, and God's rich provision for both. As the Apostle Paul writes, "Not that we are sufficient in ourselves to claim anything as coming from us. But our sufficiency is from God, who has made us sufficient as ministers of a new covenant—not of the letter but of the spirit; for the letter kills, but the Spirit gives life." (2Cor 3:5-6) Indeed, humility calls us to "bow down," to fall to our knees, to recognize our utter dependence on the Father. And to proclaim that anything good in us or from us flows out of the Father/Son/Spirit living in, working through, and empowering us in our weakness. When we ask ourselves what **our worship** should be, we should recognize both the ritual or form we use to express our worship and the lives we lead as expressions of our worship.

Micah's answer to the question "How do I worship the Lord?" may seem confusing. Micah's audience would have understood the question to be concerned with the ritual of worship that characterized their lives. They were accustomed to bringing sacrifices to the Lord; to bringing the first fruits of their labor to the Lord; to offering their possessions as payment for their sin and guilt. Their worship (remember the Hebrew word means to bow down, to humbly affirm the authority and power of the one worshipped) had been in response to the mighty works of God: He brought them up out of Egypt (6:4); He redeemed them from slavery (6:4b); He gave them leaders to look after them (6:4c); He did many great things for them (6:5). Micah tells them their Lord is angry and has a case against them. Even though they have done all the ritualistic acts expected of them or required of them in the law. He is angry because their "form" of worship (their sacrifices and offerings) is not aligned with the lives they are living with their neighbors. And even worse, their "worship" does not express a heartfelt relationship with their source of life; instead, it reflects a broken relationship.

Broken Relationships

Let's look at their sins briefly because it is important that we remember that worship flows out of our relationship with God. It is not a ritual we perform or an obligation of our faith. It is our response to the God who has called us into relationship with Him and then into a relationship with others. Sin breaks that relationship and subverts our worship.

Micah tells his people they have robbed others of what was theirs: "Am I still to forget your ill-gotten treasures." (6:10a) They have held back part of the offering they promised and have given only the "short ephah." (6:10b) This sin reveals their heart's belief that what they have is theirs and not God's. They hold back from God

3: THE SACRIFICE

perhaps out of greed or selfishness or more likely because they do not believe that God can meet their material needs. Instead of recognizing that their "sufficiency" comes from God Himself, they take it upon themselves to make sure they have enough by "robbing" God of what is rightfully His.

Also, Micah points out they lie and cheat in business (6:11) by acting in ways that benefit them at the expense of their neighbor. The first image is of a businessman whose scales for measuring the weight of what is being purchased have been rigged. Manipulated so the buyer gets less than what he is buying (the seller has more product to sell because he has cheated one buyer and can use the excess product to sell to another). Note here that this passage is a perfect example of how Hebrew uses repetition to reinforce and expand an idea or image. The latter half of the verse mentions a seller with "a bag of false weights." This seller has not rigged the scale itself but instead has created a bag of false weights: a one-ounce copper coin (looks like the real thing) is a half-ounce false coin.

Finally, Micah speaking for God accuses the people of violence and dishonesty (6:12). In short, these people do not lead lives consistent with a dependence on God. Or consistent with an acknowledgment that God is Creator and Lord of all. nor consistent with a belief that all they have is His and to be used in His service. While they "bowed down" in worship, their physical expression was not an authentic expression of their hearts before God.

No matter what we learn here about the nature of worship, we can never lose sight of the fact that worship is ultimately a response to God. And we humans respond to stimuli or to situations or to people in a wide variety of ways. Consider a couple of common ones. One response could be characterized as the response of instinct. We instinctively blink our eyes when an object approaches with speed (as kids we used to get quite a kick out of making the other blink--"made you blink!"). Another response to situations is what I would call a habit. I know people who chew their nails as a matter of habit. It is not a conscious act most of the time, simply a habitual behavior. The third response I see is the response that arises out of relationship. My seven-month-old grandson takes his first step, and I react with joy and fear (knowing increased mobility means both growth and increased opportunity to do damage or be injured). A friend loses a loved one and our response is to help--meals, baby-sitting, just being there--because the relationship demands these responses.

What response is appropriate when another person steps in front of a bullet meant for us? Or when another secures our freedom by becoming a slave in our place? Or what should our response be to one who created the incredible and beautiful world we see around us. To the God who created us to live in harmony with that beautiful natural world; who created it for us to enjoy and to care for? I believe the answer to these questions is worship, and frankly our response to these things must take on a greater scope than an activity we engage in on Sunday with other believers. It must become an expression of our life in the fullest sense. And while the richness of this idea is worth much deeper consideration, I am going to leave that for each of us to prayerfully consider.

I am concerned with our practice of worship as a community of faith, and how the Apostle Paul consistently presses the vision that worship transcends Sunday morning with its ritual and forms. He calls us to present our bodies as "living sacrifices which is *our* spiritual worship." (Rom. 12:1) Our lives themselves are to express a response to what God has done. Our lives then are to be worship. I don't know about you, but I find this idea to be more than a little daunting.

IV
The Celebration

He has made everything beautiful in its time. He has also set eternity in the hearts of men; yet they cannot fathom what God has done from beginning to end. (Ecclesiastes 3:11)

John tells us in the book of Revelation that eternity we will spend in worship. I don't know about most other believers but if my experience of worship is any indication, I am not all that excited about spending eternity worshipping. I would find discussions about the meaning of Scripture more to my liking, so I was heartened to learn of a list of spiritual temperaments (taken from <u>Sacred Pathways: Discover Your Soul's Path to God</u> by Gary Thomas) that at least gave me hope that eternity for me would be wonderful! In his book, Thomas identifies nine what he calls "temperaments" that characterize people, and I found helpful in thinking about the various forms that worship might take, depending on one's temperament. A list of these temperaments and a brief description is below. While the intellectual temperament is a good fit for me, I also recognize that there is much more to worship than my love of the study of God's Word.

- **Naturalists** love God best outdoors. These people worship amid God's creation. They celebrate His majesty and discover spiritual truths through nature.
- **Sensates** love God through their senses. These people worship through sensual experiences: sights (like art), sounds (music), smells, and more.
- **Traditionalists** love God through religious rituals and symbols. These people worship through the traditions and

sacraments of the Church. They believe structure, repetition, and rigidity, like weekly liturgy, lead to deeper understanding of God and faith.

- **Ascetics** love God in solitude and simplicity. These people worship through prayer and quiet time, and the absence of all outside noise and distraction.

- **Activists** love God through righteous confrontation, fighting for godly principles and values. They worship through their dedication to and participation in God's truth about social and evangelistic causes.

- **Caregivers** love God by serving others, and worship by giving of themselves. They may nurse the sick and disabled, "adopt" a prisoner, donate time at a shelter, etc.

- **Enthusiasts** love God through mystery and celebration. These people worship with outward displays of passion and enthusiasm. They love God with gusto!

- **Contemplatives** love God through adoration. These people worship by their attentiveness, deep love, and intimacy. They have an active prayer life.

- **Intellectuals** love God with their mind with their hearts open to a new attentiveness when they understand something new about God. These people worship through intense study, apologetics, and intellectual pursuits.

In John's vision of the throne in heaven, the twenty-four elders spend their time falling before "him who sits on the throne, and worship him who lives forever and ever." (Rev 4:9) This activity occurs whenever the living creatures give glory and honor and thanks to God, as pointed out in verse 8 is "day and night they never stop saying: 'holy, holy, holy is the Lord God Almighty, who was, and is, and is to come.'" Since eternity is going to be all about

4: THE CELEBRATION

worship and since we experience worship here and now, I believe that our worship should give us a glimpse into heaven!

(Note: I do take some heart from one little phrase here "and is to come." I expect that John's vision reflects heaven prior to Jesus' final restoration of the new Jerusalem for His people since the creatures wait in expectation. The elders on the other hand simply—or profoundly—proclaim His worthiness to receive glory and honor and power to Him in whom we have our being.)

We yearn for eternity in so many ways. The preacher writes, "He has also set eternity in the hearts of men; yet they cannot fathom what God has done from beginning to end." We long for the eternal, which will last but we fail to take advantage of an opportunity to experience the bits and pieces of eternity present in our lives today, in worship.

Jesus promised us that the Kingdom of God--an eternal kingdom ruled by the father--is ours today, not just in the future. Look at the first beatitude in Matthew chapter five: "Blessed are the poor in spirit for theirs _is_ the kingdom of heaven." Note two truths here: the new kingdom is here and now and is present among us, and it is to be experienced by those who are "poor in spirit." Being poor in spirit means recognizing that we are spiritually bankrupt (a phrase that peppered Ray Stedman's writings and teaching), that we are in desperate need of Jesus because apart from Him we are helpless. His kingdom is present with us in our daily lives, and I suspect that if we gave more thought to that reality, we might look for ways to improve our relationship with our new King. Time and time again, Jesus speaks of the dual nature of the kingdom: it is both a present reality and a future event. (Luke 17:20- "…the kingdom of God is within you.") Perhaps one of the most quoted statements about the present kingdom is from the Beatitudes where Jesus tells the crowd that "Blessed are the poor in spirit for theirs IS the kingdom of heaven." The Greek verb "is" indicates a present reality in the lives of those who recognize their poverty of spirit (i.e. their need for God and their utter dependence on Him). Jesus closes the Beatitudes by pointing to the future reality of the kingdom: "Rejoice and be glad for great is your reward in heaven." A present kingdom and a future kingdom with Him. Our present reality calls for us to begin to nurture and grow the qualities most appropriate for the future reality, to work towards worship that is true and of the spirit.

Perhaps the best-known New Testament reference to worship is Jesus' dialogue with the Samaritan woman at the well. As John records the incident, Jesus is on His way to Galilee and passes through Samaria; in fact, He goes through a town called Sychar where Jacob's well happened to be located. Early in the morning Jesus arrives at the well and sits down. When the Samaritan woman arrives, Jesus asks her for a drink, a request that surprises her, for Jews did not associate nor talk with Samaritans. And then after some conversation with this woman, Jesus hints at who He is. He suggests there is "living water." She never heard of such water, but is interested, and He tells her the time is coming when worship will neither occur on "this mountain nor in Jerusalem." Jesus then introduces her to some profound theological ideas: living water, spiritual thirst, and finally worship. Beginning with John 4: 22:

> *You Samaritans worship what you do not know; we worship what we do know for salvation is from the Jews. Yet a time is coming and has now come when the true worshipers will worship the Father in spirit and truth, for they are the worshipers the Father seeks. God is spirit, and his worshipers must worship in spirit and in truth.*

4: THE CELEBRATION

There are three remarkable things that Jesus points out here. First, Jesus tells the woman that "place" or location or geography did not matter any longer. Temples, buildings, special places, all these are going to be irrelevant and in fact already are. In place of these things, the believer's body will become the "house of worship" wherein God dwells. Consider again what Paul tells us about presenting our bodies as "living sacrifices," our spiritual form of worship! This indeed is something new and radical for God's people who have spent great sums of money, time and effort constructing and developing a life around a physical place. I wonder if the Church hasn't been a bit too quick to construct grand buildings to house Christian worship. And in so doing forgotten true worship does not need a place or a building. Is it possible that we create beautiful places and we believe they will increase our ability to worship. In fact, we create powerful obstacles to worshipping "what we know." Jesus tells the woman she's worships what "she does not know." But we believers worship a God whom we know and who knows us deeply and fully. Our great cathedrals--many architectural masterpieces filled with works of art--are monuments to our faith and love for God, but I wonder if they really do the job that we intended. Do these man-made wonders remind us of God's incredible power, holiness and majesty? Do they remind us of our weakness, our sin, and our desperate need for and dependence on Him for all that is meaningful and good? Honestly, when I have entered one of these cathedrals, my first thought goes to, "How was it possible that men built such a place?" rather than awe at the God who inspired such buildings. I am, in the silence of the place, aware men built these dazzling structures in response to what the God of the universe did in sending Jesus to us. They sought to create something beautiful for that God, and that here are "memorial altars" erected in honor of our God. Remember God's frequent command to the people of Israel to erect "markers" to remind them of what God had done. At God's command, Solomon built a grand temple to house the bread of the presence, but with His Kingdom among us, our bodies are His temple. As incredible and beautiful and powerful as these churches built to honor God appear, I wonder if they pale in comparison to a life lived in worship, a life such as Mother Teresa's?

The second thing that Jesus tells the Samaritan woman is that she acts out of ignorance. Her knowledge is incomplete at best. She worships what she does not know and furthermore what she worships does not provide salvation. Jesus connects worship with salvation in this passage. This may seem like an unusual juxtaposition—worship and salvation--but I believe there is a profound comment here on the nature of worship. Worship for a believer is inextricably tied up with salvation. What better reason to fall before God than in response to His work of salvation? What better reason to sing His praises, to adore Him, to acknowledge His greatness and to confess our sin and inadequacy than in response to the work of salvation carried out by Christ? Reviewing my experiences of worship in the Church, I wonder if we too have acted out of ignorance in the sense that we have not built our worship experiences out of the salvation event? And what would worship look like if we did just that? (More on that later.)

The third and final point Jesus makes is that true worship occurs in the human spirit, in our hearts. When He tells the woman true worship is in spirit, He does not mean some ecstatic event. Rather, He means that worship must come from the heart; it must be a response of the innermost being of a person, our spirit. God Himself is spirit, and we too are spiritual beings. Our spirit and God's spirit come together in true Christian worship. Jesus tells us that worship must be "in truth" as well. Many commentators try to develop complex, somewhat esoteric explanations of what might have been

4: THE CELEBRATION

meant by this expression. I suspect that Jesus had a relatively simple idea in mind. The gospels are filled with Jesus' criticism of the Pharisees for their hypocrisy, their inability to mean what they said and to say what they meant. They had a problem with the truth. In fact, their worship was not true at all because they did not in their hearts acknowledge God as God. So, I believe Jesus simply meant that true worship occurs when our hearts express what we mean: our actions/rituals, our words, our songs come from our spirit and express the truth of our hearts.

Note: The Greek word we translate as "worship" in the above passage is "proskulio[2]," the most frequent Greek word translated as worship in the New Testament (roughly 62 times). In essence it means to kiss (like a dog licking its master's hand); to fawn; to crouch; to prostrate oneself in homage; to do reverence; to adore. Four other Greek words are translated worship that are worth noting. "Sebomai," which means to revere or to adore, occurs four times (Matt 15:9; Mark 7:7; Acts 18:13; Rom 1:25). "Latreuo," which means to minister, serve or give service, occurs three times (Acts 7:42-43; 24:14; Phil 3:3). "Eusebeo" which means to be pious or to show respect occurs once: Acts 17:23. And "therapeus" which means to wait upon occurs one time in Acts 17:25.

At the most fundamental level, all the New Testament words for worship have a common thread; namely that worship is the response of the created to the presence of the Creator. Clearly all these expressions suggest that worship is essentially our response to the "otherness" and ultimately superiority of God in relation to us, His creation. In humility, in thanks, in recognition of His power and majesty and holiness, and in clear understanding of our own need and dependence on Him, we worship. We figuratively place ourselves before Him in abject surrender to Him.

You may have noticed my consistent emphasis on our need/dependence on our God. This emphasis is deliberate and reflects what I believe is at the core of the New Testament and Paul's teaching about who we are. I call it "need theology." We come to Jesus not because we are smart or powerful or rich but because we NEED Him, desperately and completely. We need to live with knowing our utter dependence on Him, knowing that we are not "nouns" but adjectives who are truly alive only when in relation to Him. C.S. Lewis was right when he commented the fall occurred because man wanted to be a NOUN, to stand apart on its own rather than an ADJECTIVE, which only derives meaning when connected to a noun. (In this case God Himself). II Corinthians is the heart of this message to us. We are not adequate in ourselves. God made us ministers of his love and grace. Unlike Moses hiding his face from the Israelites when the glory of God was fading, we stand in front of the world with "unveiled faces." We reflect God's glory in our weakness, in our vulnerability, and in the display of God's work in and through us. When I was in college, a singer named Pam Mark Hall wrote a wonderful song that captured this idea. One verse proclaimed, "Give me the strength to be weak so others might see You working in me." Moses to his discredit did not want to show his "weakness" and continued to hide his face for as long as he could. Instead, we're called to "with unveiled faces reflect the Lord's glory, showing the world, we are being transformed into his likeness with ever-increasing glory, which comes from the Lord, who is the Spirit." (II Cor. 3:18)

Do we in the American church attend worship on Sunday morning expecting that our "job" is to throw ourselves at the feet of God in humility and gratitude and surrender? I must confess it isn't often I

4: THE CELEBRATION

go to worship with my community of faith, conscious that what we gather to do is flatten ourselves before the mighty and holy Creator of the universe! In fact, when was the last time any of us bowed to someone out of respect? I realize Western culture glorifies independence and strength. It is unlikely that our worship will take on more robust expressions of humility. But at the least we need to consider together what it means for the church to express in action our collective humility, dependence, and creature nature before our Creator.

When God delivered the people of Israel out of Egypt, an interesting thing occurred. As the people readied to cross the Jordan into the Promised Land, Moses summoned them and gave them a stern lecture, reminding them of their time in the wilderness and the giving of the Law. In chapter 9 of the book of Deuteronomy, he assures the people that "the Lord your God is the one who goes across ahead of you like a devouring fire." Those words must have been reassuring to them, but Moses goes on to warn them about taking the credit once the dust settles:

> *After the Lord your God has driven them out before you, do not say to yourself, "The Lord has brought me here to take possession of this land because of my righteousness." Understand then, that it is not because of your righteousness that the Lord your God is giving you this good land to possess, for you are a stiff-necked people. (Deut. 9: 4-6)*

Why do you think Moses tells them they are a people with stiff necks? Is it possibly because this people do not like submitting to God (it is difficult to bow down if you have a stiff neck!)? Is it possible these people would rather believe that their success and strength and power are the result of their own abilities and skill? Is it because this people were not willing to submit themselves to the one true God while being quite willing to submit to a golden calf created by their own hands? If we look back to the account of the golden calf in Exodus 32 and 33, we will see that their reputation as being a stiff-necked people originated from their worship of the golden calf.

I believe that Scripture is warning us of our tendency to worship ourselves and the things that we create because in so doing, we set ourselves up as gods. Whether we submit our lives and our families to the demands of success in the workplace or material possessions or reputation in the community doesn't make much difference. All those things can be objects of worship if they reflect a heart unwilling to bow before God. To bow down in humility, in submission, in recognition He alone is the source of all. The source of everything we might lay claim to and any strength, ability or success we might have and which we may tend to worship in His place. When I think of lives lived in humility and submission, I think of former president Jimmy Carter and Billy Graham. Two men who showed what it is like to live in our western culture and be humble servants who seemed to always be aware of their need for their Savior.

[2] Other passages where this word is used: Matt 2:2,8; 4:9-10; 18:26; 28:9; Luke 4:8; Mark 15:19; John 12:20; Acts 7:43; 8:27; 10:25; 24:11; I Cor 14:25; Heb 1:6; Rev 3:9; 4:10;7:11-12; 9:20;11:1,16; 13:8,12,15; 14:7,9,11; 15:4; 19:4-7, 10; 22:8-9.

V

Forever His

There is no narrowing so deadly as the narrowing of man's horizon of spiritual things. No worse evil could befall him in his course on earth than to lose sight of heaven. (Inscription in Stanford Memorial Church)

This music crept by me upon the waters, Allaying both their fury, and my passion, With its sweet air. (The Tempest, I, ii, 375)

Jesus' Revelation to John is a most amazing and mysterious piece of Scripture. Within it are two chapters which I believe give us a taste of eternity and a framework with which to consider what worship in the Church ought to be like. In chapter 4, John enters heaven after a voice calls out to him saying, "Come up here and I will show you what must take place after this." He paints a picture, which I hesitate to describe here. I fear not having the skill to do any better than he has already done. Still, I think it will help us if we pause for a moment to consider the scene. In the center of the room is a throne from which comes lightning, thunder and other sense-splitting elements. Twenty-four other thrones surround the central one; an elder wearing a golden crown sits on each of the twenty-four thrones. Between the elders and the central throne are four creatures of various forms.

In heaven, John tells us, there are five songs I believe are expressions of worship, expressions of what heaven will be for us, and challenges to the church today. A challenge to begin now preparing believers for an eternity spent in worship of our God. I began by asking whether any of us can imagine spending eternity in worship. Those who can imagine so much are way ahead of the rest, because I for one am not that excited about spending eternity doing anything close to what I have often experienced in the church. On the other hand, I imagine eternity is comprised of some of the more stimulating and enjoyable aspects of life. Such as the warmth of friendship, the excitement of shooting the rapids, the joy of fellowship, the thrill of learning new things. But remember this picture is before Jesus' return and establishment of a new heaven and a new earth where we can "only imagine" what it (heaven) will be like.

John does paint a picture for us that just might have some things we could easily imagine spending great amounts of time doing. So, let's look at the five songs described in Revelation and consider how they might inform what our worship should resemble and how we might practice worship that reflects the essence of these songs. This way we can begin to enjoy the Kingdom of Heaven that is present for us here and now which in its fullness awaits us in the future.

The first song begins in Revelations 4:8 with the words:

> *Holy, holy, holy*
> *is the Lord God Almighty,*
> *who was, and is, and is to come.*

The four living creatures that surround the throne never cease to proclaim these words. For now, forget that the creatures are covered with eyes, have six wings and each resemble a different living creature. They are certainly "otherworldly" and remind us of the "otherness" of our creator. In essence, John is giving us here a picture of heaven which begins with this recognition that our God

5: FOREVER HIS

is OTHER, He is holy! In my experience, holiness is a much-abused and misunderstood concept. The root of the Hebrew word means "to be clean or pure." It is often used in context to mean consecrated, set aside, dedicated for a special purpose. The Greek roots most translated "holy" also suggest consecration, or setting aside for a special purpose, purity from defilement (sin or evil), and rightness or properness. The four living creatures in Revelation affirm with their entire being that God is Holy.

What would our lives look like if we never stopped affirming that God is holy? What does it mean for us as individuals that we serve and worship a holy God? The answer is simple. We should conduct our days in full awareness that our nature before Christ inhabited us was a sinful one. Be mindful we are wholly dependent on Him for acceptance by the Father; and that we are dependent on Him to transform us into the image of Christ. For me at least, such a view changes how I relate to those around me. I cannot claim superiority based on my own goodness or strength; I cannot withhold love or good if it is in my power to give based on a mistaken belief that I earned my position. I cannot be "stiff-necked" as Israel was. The truth is that who I am and what I have--whether material possessions, friends or family, success or reputation--flows out of the grace of a Holy God. A God who is not like the me before Christ began His transformation. It looks to me as if eternity in part will be spent affirming the holiness of God. In the Kingdom of the "now," what things prevent us from seeing or experiencing the holiness of God? For this writer, there are so many including my pride, my satisfaction with things that "I do," the log in my eye that prevents me from seeing others as God sees them. I struggle to spend time in Scripture learning about my holy God. My prayer life which all too often is consumed by my needs and wants and not an acknowledgment of my sin, and my forgetting that Jesus "died to make men holy."

With the affirmation of God's holiness, the twenty-four elders "fall down before him who sits on the throne, and **worship** him who lives forever and ever" (4:10). Isn't it interesting the elders fall. They flatten themselves before the majesty, holiness and power of God. They recognize their own unworthiness and difference from the one who sits on the throne, even though they too sit on thrones of their own. In fact, they lay their crowns before the throne and say,

> *You are worthy, our Lord and God,*
> *to receive glory and honor and power, for you created all things,*
> *and by your will they were created and have their being.*

The response of the elders is the second song John records in these chapters. It follows from the first as a response to the recognition that our God is a holy God. The elders announce that God is worthy, by virtue of His creative power, to receive glory and honor and power. I suppose that at first glance the words spoken or sung by the elders seem to state the obvious: God is God. He is the Creator of all that is. If I'm right, the elders spend a great deal of time (if there is such a thing as time in heaven) in a prone position ("fall down before him"). They are singing that God is worthy and that He is the Creator. Notice that John records that "day and night" the four living creatures never stop saying "Holy, holy, holy is the Lord God Almighty" (4:8). And whenever the living creatures give glory and honor to God, the elders "fall down before him who sits on the throne." Well, if the creatures sing out day and night God is holy, I suspect they are pretty much giving Him glory, honor and thanks. Therefore, the elders are constantly in worship. But remember here that worship is much more than their physical position before the throne; it is their heart and actions and love for Him so I seriously doubt that heaven will find us flat on our faces; rather we will be engaged in active worship with the body of believers. So our experience of worship here is a dim reflection of what it will be like in heaven. Suffice it so say that worship will be indescribable joy!

I don't know about you, but again I become a bit concerned mostly because it is difficult for me to imagine eternity spent in worship. I am beginning to believe the problem isn't that eternity isn't wonderful but my experience of worship in this life is a far cry from what it will be like on the other side.

Let's look at what the elders actually do here because I think their actions may be instructive. First, they fall on their knees. We should be used to this behavior by now as it appears in nearly every passage that we have looked at so far that has anything to do with worship. Their first act is to acknowledge by a physical action they are in the presence of God Himself, they are the creatures and He the Creator, that He is "above" them in all respects. Next, the text records they "worship him who lives forever and ever" (vs. 10). Intriguing, since the word used here for worship is "proskulio" which means among other things to prostrate oneself in homage. They have already thrown themselves to the floor in homage and now John records they "proskulio" God. I would like to suggest there is more to worship than a physical "bowing down." And the elders here have gone the next step: they have submitted their hearts, their spirits, their wills, in other words their entire selves--body, mind and spirit--to God. This act is further demonstrated by the fact they "lay their crowns before the throne." (10b) Crowns are a symbol of status, of power, and of dominion that for the believer are "on loan" from God and sanctioned by Him. Any authority or power that we gain or wield should be done as His agents and here the elders acknowledge that very fact. And so too should we, as we seek to nurture the elements of kingdom worship in the here and now, acknowledge the source and cast these "crowns" of ours before Him.

Now they "sing" that God is worthy; He is worthy of what? The elders tell us that He is worthy to receive glory. What do you think that means and why do the elders announce something that God must already know about? When we think of "glory," we most often think of it in the context of recognition or praise for work we have carried out. This is consistent with the Greek word used here. John is letting us in on a little secret. It is easy for us to give the glory to many things other than God. Consider Andre Crouch's song, "How Can I Give Thanks." A simple yet profound expression of this truth can be found in the words, "If I gain any praises let them go to Calvary." I do not find my heart of hearts often praying the praise I receive will end up being given to God for His work in and through me, but I should. If we are to live transparent, letting the world see our weakness and dependence on God and the transformation that results, then I think that our lives will in fact let the praises go to Calvary.

Next, they announce that God is worthy to receive honor. What is honor and what does it have to do with worship? We typically believe that which we honor to be of great value. Honor is often a show of respect, a recognition the person or thing being honored is somehow set apart from the rest of us by virtue of a heroic deed, special wisdom, age, or position. A life of worship is one that honors God for what He has done in our lives, we honor Him for the gift He has given to us.

Finally, our God is worthy to receive power. Now here's an unusual thought! God who is "omnipotent," which in most dictionaries means "all-powerful," can receive additional power? From where? Surely not from us. The Greek word translated in most versions as

5: FOREVER HIS

"receive" would be better translated as "take" or "get hold of." Our God is worthy to take power to Himself. Perhaps John is calling to mind Jesus who did NOT take power to Himself but rather gave that power up for our sakes. In the Kingdom, God is the only one who is worthy to claim all power and to take it to Himself, which the elders recognize and proclaim as truth.

John concludes this song by explaining simply why God is worthy: He is the Creator. It is through an act of His will that everything exists, and it is through His will that all things continue to have being. For those of you who are philosophers by nature, there is a great truth in these simple words: the essence of being human is intimately tied to the being of God. The implications are significant: separation from God is nothing other than non-being. Not a new concept if we remember Martin Buber's argument that it is in the "I-Thou" relationship that meaning exists. Not too different from Jesus' statement that "Apart from the father I can do nothing."

The third song presented by John follows the vision of the Lamb taking the scroll from the one who sat on the throne. The elders and the four living creatures fall before the Lamb this time.

Each one had a harp, and they were holding golden bowls full of incense, which are the prayers of the saints. And they sang a new song:

> *'You are worthy of taking the scroll and to open its seals, because you were slain, and with your blood you purchased men for God from every tribe and language and people and nation. You have made them to be a kingdom and priests to serve our God and they will reign on the earth.' Rev 5:8b-10*

Once again, we face the affirmation that God--in this case Jesus the Christ--is worthy. What is interesting here is the Lamb is found worthy to reveal the truth: to break the seals and to open the scroll, to reveal the names of the redeemed. I believe that it is out of this understanding of our redemption the true worshiper responds to God in worship. The Lamb purchased us with his blood. He made us into a kingdom. He made us priests to serve God, to reign on earth--most probably the "new earth" which will appear at the end of time-- and he has given us authority. We have been bought, bought with blood and consequently we belong to Him who has purchased us. It is not easy for a modern American to think of himself/herself as a commodity, as something purchased but consider this idea for a moment. How do we view the things we purchase? They are ours to do with as we please; they belong to us; we exercise authority over them, and we use them according to our plans. It is easy for us to find ourselves ensnared by other "purchasers" in our daily lives. Many of us have been purchased by our bosses; others by the views and thoughts of those around us; still others by their possessions. Some by the world's definition of success. And for many, the snare of daily life that crowds out the voice of God. A snare that crowds out time with God and crowds out any possibility that our lives might be lived FOR Him rather than for family, friends, or profession.

The Lamb has made us a kingdom; God's kingdom and it is both here and now and in the future. Should worship not reflect the kingdom to which we belong? Shouldn't our worship be directed at the King? We are, each of us, priests after the "order of Melchizedek" in the service of God. The writer of Hebrews tells us Melchizedek became a priest "not on the basis of regulation as to his ancestry but on the basis of the power of an indestructible life" (Hebrews 7:16). And so, we too are priests on the basis on Jesus' indestructible life. We are priests "forever in the order of

5: FOREVER HIS

Melchizedek" (Hebrews 7:17). The temple ritual and priestly office are, in one sense, gone. In another sense, we have become the priests whose job is to enter the holy of holies, not once a year but every moment of our lives. We are to live in the presence of God, and I suspect that living in His presence requires that our lives become an expression of worship.

Song number four occurs in verse 12:

> *"Worthy is the lamb who was slain,*
> *to receive power and wealth and wisdom and strength*
> *and honor and glory and praise."*

This song is much like the second song but with a few notable distinctions. This song affirms the deity of Christ--the Lamb-- and introduces several new aspects to worship. This song is directed at the Lamb who is clearly one and the same as the one who sits on the throne and lives forever. But the interesting change here is that in addition to affirming God is worthy to receive glory, honor and power, this song affirms there are three other aspects of human life. Aspects that also belong to God: wisdom, wealth and strength. It is also interesting to note that it is the angelic host singing this song, not the elders who surround the throne. The angelic host sings out the Lamb is the source of strength and wisdom and wealth. These are important affirmations for me amid American culture. I do not often view my own smarts as the result of God's grace; often I view them as the result of my own hard work, study and effort. My strength is also the consequence of my hard work and effort. Or is it? How easy it is to forget that even my health, my body's ability to fend off infection, genetic factors, all are out of my control, subject to the hidden working of the Creator. This fourth song of the angels reminds us our debt to Him is all encompassing; we owe all to Him and His work in and through us in the world. His is true wisdom and strength and from Him comes any wealth that we have. How different would our lives be if we truly viewed ourselves this way? How much easier would it be to forgive others, to share what we have with those less fortunate, and to walk in humility with our fellow creatures and before our holy and loving God?

The fifth and final song recorded in John's letter begins in verse 13. John tells us that every creature in heaven and on and under earth or on the sea takes part in this song. In the first song, it is the four living creatures who sing. In the second it is the elders who shout their praises. In the third it is the creatures and the elders together. In the fourth we hear tens of thousands of angels sing God's praises; and in the fifth song, it is the whole of creation who sings praise to God the Creator. All creation sings of God's power and honor and glory "forever and ever." And the elders fell and worshipped.

What John reveals here are several aspects of worship the modern church frequently forgets. First, worship is God-directed. The elders and heavenly hosts sang their praises to Him; not to one another, not to some other audience. Theirs was not a performance for a "seen" audience; theirs was a performance before the King of Kings. To God and God alone is worship to be directed. Secondly, the content of worship is made up of two important elements. The first of these is an affirmation of our dependence on God--our creatureliness, our need for Him, and our sinfulness. The second element of worship which John presents here is that worship is our response to who He is and what He has done--praise and adoration. Worship as it is portrayed here is simply us in the presence of God, "naked and unashamed" in all our creatureliness, responding to everything that God is: His power and glory and authority to be sure, also His love and forgiveness and acceptance, and finally His redemptive and creative work within us. We might do well to remember Jesus words to the disciples after He was anointed by a "sinful" woman (Luke

7:36-47). He reminds them that there is a connection between the love demonstrated by the woman and the depth of forgiveness she experienced: "He who has been forgiven little loves little." She responded to the Lord out of the profound awareness of what it meant to be totally forgiven for a life of sin. I struggle remembering my own sin before Him as I find success in life and relationships. It is wise for us to continuously ask Him to teach us of our sin and need for a Savior. Are we aware of our own sin and failure? How should we, who have been forgiven of truly deep sin, respond to the God who calls us to Himself?

John Hankerson

VI

My Worship

So long as man remains free, he strives for nothing so incessantly and so painfully as to find someone to worship. (Dostoyevsky, The Brothers Karamazov)

Plunged in thy depth of mercy let me die. The death that every soul that lives desires. (Cowper, Madame Guion)

The death that "every soul that lives desires" is the death of self, offered in the call of Christ: "Whoever tries to keep his life will lose it, and whoever loses his life will preserve it" (Luke 17:33). Worship is the only proper response I can make to my Creator, redeemer, and holy God. It is my acknowledgment of His character, His otherness, His "Godness," and His claim over me. It is a wholehearted admission of my NEED for Him and my place in relation to Him. It is my first and last response to His goodness and holiness, my confession, my PRAISE, my expression of thanks and humble adoration.

There is a passage in the letter to the Hebrews that summarizes much of what I have discussed so far. It is worth looking at before we consider what it means to worship as part of a community of faith in the 21st century.

Beginning in chapter 12 and verse 18, we discover a contrast that characterizes our relationship with the Father and therefore should characterize our worship.

For you have not come to what may be touched. To a blazing fire, and darkness, and gloom, and a tempest, and the sound of a trumpet, and a voice whose words made the hearers entreat that no further messages be spoken to them. For they could not endure what was given, "If even a beast touches the mountain, it shall be stoned." Indeed, so terrifying was the sight that Moses said, "I tremble with fear." But you have come to the city of the living God, the heavenly Jerusalem, and to innumerable angels in festal gathering. You've come to the assembly of the firstborn who are enrolled in heaven. And to a judge who is God of all, and to the spirits of just men made perfect. And to Jesus, the mediator of a new covenant, and to the sprinkled blood that speaks more graciously than the blood of Abel. (Heb. 12:18-24 ESV)

The people of Israel approached God with fear, with a degree of distance and with a sense of the mysterious. They came to a mountain where they were told not to touch ("They cannot come up to Mount Sinai, for thou thyself didst charge us, saying, 'Set bounds about the mountain, and consecrate it.'" (Ex. 19:23, 26 RSV); that mountain burned with fire and was covered in darkness, gloom and storm. ("On the morning of the third day there was thunder and lightning and a thick cloud upon the mountain, and a loud trumpet blast so that all the people trembled. Ex.19:16). The voice of God was like a trumpet blast so loud that those who heard begged that it be silenced it was so terrible. Moses' own words were, "I am trembling with fear" (Deut. 9:19). The people's response was indeed worship but of a different kind from ours. It was a response born from awe and fear and limited understanding. In Christ, God built a bridge to us that sheds light on things hidden, taking away fear ("perfect love casts out all fear"), drawing each of us into the presence of the living God. It is God's perfect love that sanctified

6: MY WORSHIP

you and me and removed the punishment for our sin and cast out all fear!

The writer of Hebrews tells us that we have come to "Mount Zion, to the heavenly Jerusalem, the city of the living God. To thousands upon thousands of angels in joyful assembly, to the church of the firstborn, whose names are written in heaven."

But what do these rather unusual things have to do with us, Christians in America at the beginning of the twenty-first century? The writer tells us we've come to the city of the living god, not to a sterile, cold, foreboding rock--not to a mountain--but to a city. It is a place where there is life and community; it is the city where our God dwells. Our life as a community of faith is a life lived in the city of God where we, always in His presence, should give Him worship, honor and praise. We inhabit the city of God, the city where angels forever sing joyful songs of praise. What an image! Do you experience this on a day-today basis? Do you even seek to see your life here from such a perspective? I suspect that for most of us our day-to-day lives are a far cry from an experience of walking in the City of God. Our "city" is probably quite different. Our city is filled with traffic, honking horns, hurried and angry people, crime, waste and often death. The writer to the Hebrews insists we have arrived at a new city. I believe it is important for us to consider just what he meant and how that should influence our individual worship.

What kinds of things characterize a city today? Are the characteristics only those mentioned above: crime, overcrowding, smog, traffic, concrete, and other features commonly found in our big cities? Or are there other qualities of cities that are more abstract and perhaps more relevant to the frame of reference that the writer to the Hebrews was using: things like interdependence, interaction, and communication. Cities are a virtual web of relationships that influence and infect nearly every aspect of a city-dweller's life. Writers often speak of the "heartbeat" of the city as if each city has its own character, its own unique personality. If the heartbeat and personality of a city are what is meant in Hebrews, then we must ask ourselves a couple of questions: "Does the world look at our 'city' and see a city with a unique character, a 'heartbeat' all its own, and do they see Jesus in that heartbeat or something else?" "Does our community of faith resemble the City of God?" Before I attempt an answer to this question, I need to make an important observation: I believe worship is the "heartbeat" of the city of God filling us with life, pumping the living water throughout the body, and that draws each member of the body together into the whole. When we, as members of the church, the body of Christ, are not engaged in worshipping in "spirit and in truth," we cannot make real here on earth the presence of the City of God.

What should the City of God look like and how do we, God's people, live in this new city? We know from Scripture already that my worship should:

- Affirm His authority and power and glory
- Recognize my dependence on God for everything
- Recognize that without God's active involvement in my life and without my constant dependence on Him, I cannot be holy as He has called me to be
- Recognize my own sin and therefore live in humility with others, not judging others but seeing in others a person whom God loves and died for
- Openly declare my praise to God

6: MY WORSHIP

The five attributes of God's people identified above should be the church's "worship manifesto," and as such they should be dominant characteristics of the behavior of people in the City of God. Worship is expressing to God our acknowledgement of His power and glory as we openly confess our absolute dependence on Him for life, love and grace. We affirm His holiness and our need to be connected to Him, the source of all good, living openly before others. We do this so they might see God at work in us and praising, thanking and loving Him in song, word and deed.

As His body here on earth and as dwellers in His City, our lives are to be characterized by praise, thanksgiving, recognition of God's "God-ness," and acknowledgment of our need and dependence. These are what should characterize our lives in His city.

Furthermore, this "City of God" in which we dwell is filled with thousands of angels who dwell there with us, angels dressed in clothes suitable for a great party (Heb 12: 22). This is a joyful city, a city that rejoices in the work of its king, a city that celebrates new life. The community of faith is to be a joyful group; we are to celebrate together because God has done wondrous things! Where should this celebration occur? Everywhere but definitely in our acts of individual and communal worship! Our worship should reflect this celebratory quality; our worship must always be a celebration. We celebrate foremost what God has done for us in Christ:

> *"While we were yet helpless, at the right time Christ died for the ungodly." (Rom. 5:6 RSV)*

How did the lame man that Peter healed respond? With celebration, so much celebration that he shames us who have so much more than physical healing to celebrate.

> *"And leaping up he stood and walked and entered the temple with them, walking and leaping and praising God." (Acts 3:8 RSV)*

Over and over, we see in the Psalms of David a call to celebration, to rejoicing in our God, not only when things are going well but in all circumstances. We see David surrounded by enemies on all sides sing out "Let the righteous rejoice in the Lord" (Psalm 64:10), "May all who seek you rejoice and be glad in you" (Psalm 70:4). We have reasons to rejoice; our God is at work in our world and in our city to accomplish His will, even when that will is not clear to us:

> *"You crown the year with your bounty, the tracks of your chariot drip with fatness. The pastures of the wilderness drip, the hills gird themselves with joy, the meadows clothe themselves with flocks, the valleys deck themselves with grain, they shout and sing together for joy." (Psalm 65:13 ESV)*

What have we learned from the writer to the Hebrews? First, not only here in this passage but throughout Scripture we see that worship must be celebratory. We must build in a sense of celebration, of rejoicing and affirming the good and mighty works of God. In American individualistic culture, celebrating the mighty works of God must start with a recognition of what God has done for us personally and then an affirmation of what He has done for the church. I need to be reminded that I have been redeemed, that I was caught in sin, that in the cross I found new life. That kind of reminder is not always easy. Not many of us like to be reminded of where we have come from or how much we have changed. In fact, I suspect we rather enjoy not being reminded because then we can in small ways start to take credit for the change that has occurred. We can take some pride in what good people we are. Pride in how

6: MY WORSHIP

much we give in time and money to the cause of God; we can begin to see others as "less mature," as "weaker" brothers or sisters whom we should support in prayer. How easy it is to be ensnared by a false pride of accomplishment even in the church: "I pulled myself up by my bootstraps, I chose the right path and look where it has gotten me!" Paul agrees that we need to boast but suggests our boasting should be that we know Jesus, the author and giver of the life of love and forgiveness that is ours. He is the author of the life that is changed from one degree of glory into another, all for Him. We need to be reminded that it is God's grace that has brought us "safe thus far and grace will lead us home." Our new birth, our transformation from one degree of Christlikeness to another is a work, not ours but God's. "He who began a good work in you will bring it to completion in the day of Christ Jesus." The church needs to be a place where the strong and the weak, saints and sinners, rich and poor, stand alongside one another. Each sincerely saying, "We are equally valued and loved by the Father and by one another and by the church."

The community of faith needs to remind itself that being a body--a topic for the next chapter--implies that all members from the worldly rich to the worldly poor are needed, valued and loved.

> *"For there is no distinction; since all have sinned and fall short of the glory of God, they are justified by his grace as a gift, through the redemption which is in Christ Jesus." (Rom. 3:22-23 ESV)*

The Hebrews passage continues by listing those with whom we share the heavenly city: we find ourselves part of the "church of the firstborn whose names are written in heaven." Incredible! Through the power and love and work of the "firstborn" whom we know to be Jesus, our names are already written in heaven. This fact is a further cause for celebration: our names are in heaven. We belong there; it is our home!

We have come to the heavenly city, into the presence of others: innumerable angels, the assembly of the firstborn and now to a judge "who is God of all." Lest we become too rambunctious in our celebrating this new life that is ours, we are reminded gently that we live our lives now in the presence of the judge who is "God of all." Our judge is God of all, not just the presiding judge over a small claims court. He is the God of all, everything that is, a universe so vast that its size alone is beyond our comprehension. He is God of all, and He is a holy God. We stand in the presence of God, the judge of all men. Yet, the writer tells us that we also have come "to the spirits of righteous men made perfect" and to Jesus who has provided a new covenant. We have nothing to fear from this powerful and holy God because He made us perfect through His power; He has established a new agreement with us, His covenant; He has made us His people. The writer finishes with the following powerful words:

> "Therefore, since we <u>are receiving</u> a kingdom that cannot be shaken, <u>let us be thankful</u>, and so worship God <u>acceptably</u> with <u>reverence and awe</u>, for our God is a consuming fire." (Heb. 12:28-29 RSV).

We are given a kingdom that will withstand all the forces of evil that come against it. It is not subject to overthrow; it will not be taken from us; its king will never lose His power over this kingdom, nor will we be sent away for failure to do our part. God's redemptive and transforming power in us ushers in this kingdom. Note the verb used is in a tense that implies ongoing action: "are receiving." We are continually receiving more and more of this kingdom as God's will is made real in our lives and as we are transformed into His image. This process is inexorable! And our response should be one of thanksgiving: "let us be thankful." Our worship must be characterized by thankfulness towards God. He is the object of our worship, the audience for our praise and thanks and our coming together in worship must embrace a spirit of thanksgiving. It is out of thankful hearts that we begin to worship God "acceptably." The passage is clear: be thankful and SO worship God acceptably. Thanksgiving is at the heart of acceptable worship. Now why might that be? What about thankfulness that is so essential? Two things: thanksgiving flows out of a sense that I--the one giving thanks--am beholden to another. I have received that which I did not provide for myself. I have been given a gift and the greater the gift, the greater my gratitude. In our thanks, we acknowledge that God has acted in ways that have made us indebted to Him, that He has done for us things that we were powerless to do for ourselves. Secondly, thanksgiving is our admission that God is God. It is our admission that we are the receivers of a gift and in this case, a gift that reveals our need and dependence on God, the giver. He has redeemed us, provided for us, and consequently has a claim on our lives. What do you find your heart celebrating or giving thanks for naturally? Have you had or are you in a season where it is hard to be grateful to God or to others? What has contributed to that season?

Our worship is also to be characterized by "reverence and awe." The Greek word used here contains the idea of downcast eyes. Revering God is humility before Him. It is recognizing He is the holy one; as before, it is bowing down before Him, submitting ourselves to Him, proclaiming that He is the Creator and we are the creatures! The word translated here as "awe" might best be thought of as a profound caution in the presence of power beyond imagining. The Greek implies demeanor appropriate in the presence of the King of Kings and Lord of Lords. Repeatedly we are seeing in the Scriptures that our worship is to reflect our recognition of God's majesty and holiness and power. In how many of our churches today do we see people bowing down before their Creator? In how many evangelical places of worship is Sunday morning a time where God's people gather to give worship. Gathering to give Him praise, adoration, thanksgiving, all recognizing that He is God and we are His creation and a sinful one at that.

Our worship must flow from thanksgiving; it must be reverent, and it must be characterized by a devotion that flows out of a contrite heart. Why? Because "our God is a consuming fire." As fire literally consumes--completely takes--the essence of the wood that is burning, God demands everything from us. Our worship must reflect our total surrender of all that we are to him as fire demands all from the wood.

The writer of Hebrews takes us on a 'faith journey" beginning in chapter 1 and culminating in the final chapter, reminding us of where we have been and where we have arrived: "Through Jesus, therefore, let us continually offer to God a sacrifice of praise—the fruit of lips that confess His name. And do not forget to do good and to share with others, for with such sacrifices God is pleased" (Heb. 13:15-16). It is worth your time to read through the book of Hebrews in a single sitting to experience the incredible expanse of God's work throughout history.

What do these things mean to me and my personal worship of my God? For I do not believe that worship is ONLY reserved for the gathering of the church but rather it is also a response of each of our hearts to our Savior and our God. For me personally, these are what should characterize individual times of worship:

- Remembrance of what God has done for me

6: MY WORSHIP

- Humbly bowing down before the Creator of the universe
- Acknowledgment that I continue to need Him because I continue to sin and be broken in this world
- Confession of my brokenness and of my need. (I cannot say it often enough we must let Him show how much and deeply we need Him, how much our lives—with a capital "L"—are utterly dependent on His grace, mercy and love)
- Thanksgiving for saving me and restoring me into a relationship with Him as a son and as a friend
- Thanksgiving for all that I have and an affirmation that it is ALL His
- Praise for His work in my life and in the life of those I love

Psalm 51 is worth reading in its entirety at this point for it shows our condition and God's love and mercy in a beautiful and powerful way.

David calls out to the Lord, admitting his fallen nature— "surely I have been a sinner from birth"—and then asks God to create in him a "pure heart." He then states something that has run throughout this text so far: that what God wants from us is a "broken spirit, a broken and contrite heart." These things arise from awareness of who God is and who we are in relation to Him and in response our tongues "will sing of your righteousness" and our mouths will "declare his praise."

But worship is more than personal experience of a relationship with God; it is a communal activity as Scripture so clearly describes in all the passages examined so far. What does communal worship look like?

John Hankerson

VII

Our Worship

Therefore, with Angels and Archangels, and with all the company of heaven, we laud and magnify thy glorious Name; evermore praising thee. (The Book of Common Prayer)

The pressure in our culture to be autonomous, to exist independently apart from community is strong. This pressure extends into our life together as believers in our neighborhood churches, into our communities of faith. The writers of the New Testament couldn't have imagined the extent we can live isolated lives because of technology. But they did have a deeply rooted belief the Christian life was a life lived with one another, not separate or isolated. In one of my favorite examples of this thinking, the Apostle Peter establishes an ontological foundation for our life as a community. What I mean is that he asserts that our essence as believers, our very being, is tied up in a communal identity. Look at 1 Peter 2:9-10 RSV

> *"But you are a chosen race, a royal priesthood, a holy nation, God's own people, that you may declare the wonderful deeds of him who called you out of darkness into his marvelous light. Once you were no people but now you are God's people; once you had not received mercy but now you have received mercy."*

This Scripture begins with a declaration of our ethnicity! It does not identify our race by skin color or geographic origin. So, while God created every race, every skin color, every human trait and He declared them "good," here we see a new take on the idea of "race."

The writer identifies our race using an unusual criterion: relationship with God! We are a chosen race; at the heart of who we are (in our genes if you will) is our relationship to God Himself. He has chosen us and as a result we are a uniquely identifiable group of people. Just as the races populating our globe have distinguishing physical features--skin color, hair, physical attributes--God's people are--as Webster defines race. The definition goes as this: a division of mankind possessing traits transmissible by descent and sufficient to characterize it as a distinct human type. What traits do you think distinguish the children of God from other races? Certainly not skin color or other genetic characteristics; rather we possess one profoundly distinct characteristic: we have been born again. The old nature that was condemned to death has been regenerated by the power of the Spirit. That which is truly us has been transformed. We are related to one another as members of God's family. This is because in and through the power of the Holy Spirit, God has "fathered" a new creation in us. We share the same father who has begun a most amazing work in us.

The next declaration speaks to our vocation. We are a "royal priesthood." Both words here are significant. We serve the King of Kings and hence Peter's use of the word "royal." But our job is that of priesthood. At the most elemental level, the role of the priest is to bring the word of God to others, a role here that is not reserved for individuals but for the community of believers. It is a priesthood of believers, not the designation of a single priest.

Socially and politically speaking, Peter declares us to be a holy nation. We are holy in the sense that we are set apart, and a nation to remind us that we are to live our lives in the context of other people. What do nations do? Often, today we see nations waging war against other nations and even against their own people. Nations use their power and might to influence the direction of world affairs; nations can wield their power for good or for ill, though often nations act with decided self-interest. Nations are usually defined by geographic boundaries. But the nation of God is not like other nations. It crosses geography and races and calls believers to recognize that their allegiance is to a heavenly king whose kingdom is in the heart and whose rule knows no physical constraints. We are "God's own people"! **We** belong to Him! Not just individually but all of us collectively and it is through all of us living as a community that we can declare to the world how awesome our God is. Look at the phrasing in the verse. We are a chosen race, a royal priesthood, a holy nation, God's own people SO THAT together we might be the **Word of God** to the world. Our first job is to declare—be His WORD--His wonderful deeds. That sounds like worship to me!

Let me suggest the world will find itself drawn to Him and His people when it sees us doing what He has called us to do: worship Him. This worship must be a community event. It is well and good to spend time alone in our "prayer closets," but we are called to live as a community. And it is the community that reflects the fullness of God's love to others. Each of us has a role and a unique place in this community, a community that Christ Himself calls His Body. He is the image of the Father just as this body now reflects the image of the father to the world. What we do and who we are as a church matters! History provides ample evidence of how much the world looks at the church and remembers what it has done (or failed to do!). From the crusades and the inquisition to the silence in Germany as Hitler extended his power, the church has not always been an effective witness to God's love and grace. The world remembers and links this church with the God we worship. We do well to be aware that our life together sends a message to the world around us.

Worship is one activity we engage in as His people that others can witness and through which others can come to understand something of our God. Our response to Him—which is what worship is supposed to be—should reveal deep insight into His nature. Our celebration announces the joy, freedom, grace and the new beginnings we find in Him. Our gratitude reflects our awareness of how much He has given to us. And our praise and adoration make it clear to the world that He is God, and we have recognized our place as His subjects. We—the people of God—have been called out of darkness into light and that event should be cause for great celebration and rejoicing!

The Apostle Paul picks up this theme in his letter to the church at Ephesus: "And in him you too are being built together to become a dwelling in which God lives by his Spirit" (Eph 2:22). We are being fashioned into a holy temple, with other believers. This place that God inhabits is often referred to as His body the church. I have long suspected that we experience God more fully in relationship and worship with others and this passage seems to imply something along those lines. In the temple (which is us His church), priests of old would go and worship and bring gifts and declare the power and might and holiness of their God. The temple is the place where believers **worship**. Today, when we, His church, gather, God is present among us: the model described by the Old Testament writers suggests our gathering must be characterized by worship because where the temple is, worship must happen. God himself is among us and the only response appropriate for people brought out of darkness into light, for people who have experienced the "Christ event," for people who have tasted the love and transforming power of God in their lives, is worship.

Consider whether you see Christ more fully in community or in your personal quiet time? Most of us will probably argue that we

7: OUR WORSHIP

experience God more deeply when we are alone, in our prayer closets. But don't be fooled! Scripture suggests the fullness of God's presence resides in His body, the church! I don't want to suggest that we abandon these much-needed times of prayer and devotion, but I do believe that it is through the community of faith that God reveals himself most fully to us. Paul tells the Corinthians that "you show that you are a letter from Christ. Written not with ink but with the Spirit of the living God." The church is a letter from God to others revealing the work and power of the saving work of Christ. In Colossians, Paul writes:

> *"Let the word of Christ dwell in you richly as you teach and admonish one another with all wisdom, and as you sing psalms, hymns and spiritual songs with gratitude in your hearts to God." (Colossians 3:16 ESV)*

Our gathering should be flavored with opportunities to call one another into closer relationship with God and with praise and gratitude.

I wonder if most of us go to church on Sunday morning to experience our personal worship time but not necessarily to experience the joy of sharing worship with those around us. Are there things in our Sunday morning event that make it an individual "group" event?

What can we do to make our Sunday morning experience a community event rather than a gathering of individuals who autonomously experience something of God but do not share that experience collectively? To think about this, I go back to things I know, things that I have experienced with groups of people. I had a profound experience in college when I attended Peninsula Bible Church where every Sunday evening there was a community experience called "Body Life." Ray Stedman has written a book about this "service" but what struck me most about it was the people there shared their needs, praise and struggles. And then the "body" prayed for them with many participating. It was an incredibly moving experience to be together, sharing our brokenness and being supported and affirmed and pointed to the King who was there to meet our needs.

Another common group experience that most of us share is a sporting event. Going to a high school or college football game (or maybe even a professional sporting event) can be an exhilarating social experience. Amazing isn't it that we can have such a wonderful experience of being a community at such a secular, most superficial event!

There are several ingredients that I believe facilitate the community-like experience of these activities. Don't get me wrong! I don't believe worship should be built around sporting events as a model, but for some reason, the secular community often recognizes deep truths about the human spirit we in the church fail to notice.

The first thing I notice about sporting events is that many of the members in the crowd know why they are there: they have come to support and cheer their team. They share a common purpose that is accepted long beforehand and everyone who buys a ticket enters expecting that there will be a game and they will participate spontaneously in that game. The spectators do not come expecting to hear a speech, observe an event different from the one advertised, or be taught calculus: they come expecting to watch a game played between two teams. Christians on the other hand come to worship on Sunday morning with varying expectations. Some come to be

7: OUR WORSHIP

taught, others to socialize, still others to feel part of a wider community, and maybe even some come expecting to worship with other believers.

Our first problem as a worshiping church is that nobody knows or is willing to identify what we are doing in the pews (or chairs) Sunday after Sunday. We come, sometimes in droves, but our gathering is not characterized by a common expectation or understanding of what it is that we are doing. I would go even one step farther and argue that we do not share a common frame of reference for what worship is. That lack of shared understanding is akin to bringing British and American fans into a stadium promising to have a football game. To the British, football is what we call soccer. Boy, would they be surprised to arrive expecting soccer and getting a pointed ball, goalposts, and pads. Magnify this tenfold and you have our Sunday morning worship event. Three-hundred people with twenty, thirty, or forty different concepts of what Sunday morning should be. I challenge you to ask people why they attend Sunday service, what they expect it to be. After they have answered these questions, consider asking what they believe worship is. You will discover that we don't share common definitions or expectations. The absence of "shared expectations" makes it difficult for the community to experience shared worship!

The second difficulty in creating a community worship experience in America today is that we do not share even a simple definition of the word "worship." For some, worship is watching a minister or priest perform specified rituals and assisting in these rituals at times by speaking together words of common prayer or words of institution; for others, worship is singing. At the ball game, everyone shares a common understanding of what it means to cheer. You do not hear "boos" ringing out from fans of the team when the team is doing well. You do not see fans sitting silently in their seats when the game is close and their team is on the verge of an important play. In fact, here in the place where I live, Seattle, you see fans initiating spontaneous bursts of support in what is called "the wave." It is so well understood that fans on separate levels of our stadium time the wave so the entire group is in motion at the appropriate time. Shared understanding is important, and sports fans share some simple understandings that enable them as a group to experience a game as a "body." We in the church in contrast do not share even the simplest understanding of what worship is. Any shared understanding that might exist is often the result of tradition and experience and not consistent with Scripture's picture of worship: celebratory, participative, God-directed, and characterized by "bowing down," thanks, praise, and adoration.

Beyond not sharing a common understanding of worship, we don't even know the "rules of the game" on Sunday morning. I must confess that I have never been to a church where there is an explanation--printed or otherwise--that would help me understand both what we are doing and why we are doing it. Many good things happen in a worship service but few people in the congregation have a clue to what is going on or why. We sing hymns here or a praise chorus there; interspersed are some Scripture verses or a prayer or two. But does the order make sense to those in attendance? Is there even a plan in the order or have we merely done what we have always done? Is there a script which would help us know the purpose of our gathering, the nature of our community activities, and most important of all, "when are we supposed to cheer"?

Much of our liturgy (by liturgy I mean a form or formulary according to which public religious worship is conducted) and music has been passed down to us from those who have gone before us. It reflects the depth and devotion of saints in the church, many of whom gave their lives to the Lord. But why hasn't the church asked itself whether this liturgy still makes sense for His church today? Where did these hymns come from? If we push things back far enough, eventually we must admit the church body had to create most of it on their own. Hymns had to be written out of the experience of believers; forms of worship had to be developed which reflected the style and character of the community and culture. Local bodies of believers today should be about the business of creating their own liturgies within the biblical definition of worship! Our liturgies of worship did not originate in divine revelation; they do not carry the weight of the words of Paul or Moses; our hymns are not prescribed by scriptural text. On the contrary, our hymns and songs and spiritual songs should reflect the experience of our community with the risen Lord. To the degree that we can learn from and share in the experiences and responses of those Christians before us, we should take advantage. But their faith is theirs! We must take on the responsibility of crafting our response of faith and worship in the context of our community and culture and always considering the teaching of Scripture. But we must take up the charge!

I believe we in the church are too comfortable resting on the past. We rely on what was done before us rather than crafting out of our faith OUR OWN response of worship. Worshiping with hymns and songs and spiritual songs, OUR OWN community liturgies, rooted in Scripture foremost and connected to those saints who have gone before. We have much to learn from the great cloud of witnesses that preceded us, but the Church is alive today and dynamic. We often behave as if the church is a mausoleum for dead saints and the old ways. Our Lord is a living Lord, and it is He that is with us till the end of the age, not Paul or Peter or Luther or Calvin. Their faith matters and there is much we can learn from them and learn we should. But it is the living Lord we worship, and we worship Him not in the 18th century or even the early 20th century. We worship him now, in the time and place where His people gather. Our worship should reflect the biblical principles described earlier but our worship should also reflect the symbols, ways of communicating and culture of our communities.

We desperately need to develop the structures in our churches that would allow worship to be more fully a community experience. I would suggest the structure include a few of the things presented so far: confession, acts of thanksgiving, communal prayer, praise and adoration, and hearing God's word. Doing so will not guarantee that worship is transformed into a shared experience of believers, but it will be an important start. The very nature of sharing requires there be some form of community and in those churches where community does not exist on a person-to-person level, community worship will be difficult. True, we are all part of God's larger community. Just as football fans don't know one another and yet share in the "experience" of the game, so too can we share in the experience of God. Even though we do not know our neighbor. We share something more profound than a love for a game though; we share a love for and a relationship with the Creator of the universe. Such a common bond should bring total strangers together in wonderful ways. Nonetheless, the church should not neglect the building up of community among its members to deepen and enrich the experience of shared worship on Sunday mornings.

VIII

Culture Matters

> *If you praise him in the private language of tongues, God understands you but no one else does, for you are sharing intimacies just between you and him. But when you proclaim his truth in everyday speech, you're letting others in on the truth so they can grow and be strong and experience his presence with you. (I Cor 14: 1-2 from* <u>The Message</u> *by Eugene Peterson)*

The fourteenth chapter of Paul's letter to the church at Corinth contains several principles relevant to our consideration of worship in the twenty-first century. This is a familiar chapter to most and a controversial one when it comes to consideration of the gifts of the Spirit. Though Paul focuses on using tongues in worship, consider the nature of his argument against certain uses of tongues to make a point about language and music in our worship today. Paul begins this chapter by laying a foundational principle for the way we are to live our lives. He points out the person who speaks in tongues speaks "not to men but to God...he utters mysteries with his spirit" (vs 2). In contrast, the one who speaks a prophecy "speaks to men for their strengthening, encouragement and comfort" (vs 3). He then makes a crucial point: he wants believers to experience the gifts (in this case, to speak in tongues) but he believes the gift of prophecy is the greater gift. Why? Because the church is built up when the body can understand what is being spoken by the Spirit using a *tongue*. In other words, we are drawn into God's presence when we both hear and understand.

You may wonder how this principle is relevant to worship. In verses eleven and twelve, Paul provides further clarification: "If then I do not grasp the meaning of what someone is saying (or singing), I am a foreigner to the speaker. And he is a foreigner to me...try to excel in the gifts that build up the church." If our worship is constructed so it is as if a foreign language is being spoken, haven't we failed to build up the church?

First, the language that is part of our worship. I was raised Roman Catholic, and when I was young, Latin was the language of worship. Few people in the congregation knew Latin—most could pronounce the words, but few knew their meaning. Is there a place for conducting our worship in a language the people do not know? I do not believe so. As a parent I am acutely aware that my children sometimes speak in a language that sounds foreign to me. Expressions such as: *we schooled them, Wuz up? Sick, Dope, LOL, OMG*--do not always communicate much to me. My relationship with my children is weakened when I cannot understand their language. In their case, a simple request for a translation usually bridges the gap but we parents know the language divide is real and sometimes troubling. We believers fill our gatherings with our own language that is just as foreign to outsiders (and perhaps even to our children!). How is it possible for us as a community to join in worship when we create barriers among us by our language? Our relationships are fragile enough with one another. We have little time to devote to developing intimate relationships with others in our community because of our busy lives. Lives filled with soccer games, baseball games, school, work, house and yard work, ministry, and more. We need to exercise great care that our language in the body does not separate us from one another and from those on the outside of our fellowship.

8: CULTURE MATTERS

On that note, I suspect that there are several possible "languages" that might be worth purging from our worship. Consider with me some of the following:

- Religious jargon
- Highly intellectual language
- Formal, "ritualized" language, or ancient language

What constitutes jargon? Have you ever had a consultation with a physician whose every fourth word was a piece of medical jargon that medical students would understand but which sounded like Greek to you? What about those folks who are highly competent in the programming and use of computers and other highly technical machines? They too have a language that is their own. They talk of bits and bytes and USB ports and fire walls and Trojan viruses. And those are the easy ones! If you are anything like me, when I am in those circumstances, I feel left out, I feel stupid and inferior. My feelings of alienation arise because the language itself excludes me from participating with them in the conversation. There are many such words of jargon in the church, words and phrases, and even ideas foreign to our world today, and foreign to the world our children inhabit in their schools. It troubles me that we are not more careful to hear worship as our children hear it and ask whether we exclude them by our very words. Shouldn't we be sensitive to our kids if to no one else? Think about these expressions as examples.

> *"Washed in the blood": a visual image probably distasteful to most Americans today. Even more important than the potential unease such an expression might engender. Does this expression mean anything in modern culture? Can an unchurched individual or even a youth with limited exposure to the gospel find a way to translate the words into something*

that makes sense? I doubt it. Even more troubling is that this kind of language will never draw others to the gospel. When we use words to communicate, those words are symbols for concepts or images or experiences shared among us.

When I use the word "table" or "house," those around me have little difficulty of translating the words into a picture of some kind. Their version of table could be small or grand, but the "function" of a table is easily understood. For most Americans, washed is easily translated but the connection between being washed and blood is not. Should we use such language when it is not meaningful to those around us? It has meaning for those of us who have personally experienced the life changing power of Jesus in our lives. But can we find a new image or at least a way of talking about its meaning that communicates a relevant and understandable idea to people today? I believe we can. We need to seriously take the challenge to translate the work of Christ into the twenty-first century. When Jesus walked the earth, the church practiced blood sacrifice and ritual cleansing; even the pagan community understood the idea of a substitutionary sacrifice. Today's world does not. Even within our churches are many who have not been raised in a tradition that reinforced these symbols or metaphors of our faith.

Words like "sanctified," "propitiation," "redemption," "and "justification" are common Christian jargon. But they are also profound concepts and for the most part need translation into ideas that others outside the church in our culture can understand. Even on Sunday mornings we need to be aware of the jargon that we use. We need to do this, for no one else but the children. As a former teacher, I know well the impact that language has on our children and our youth. And I know how often I sat in church and worried

8: CULTURE MATTERS

that my own children would be turned off by what they heard, if for no other reason that it sounded foreign to them in their life and experience. No one will deny children and youth should be stretched in their understanding. That is how they grow up. I wonder if we do them a disservice, when we speak of the most important things in their (and our) lives using words and images that make little or no connection. How is it that they can see our faith is reasonable if they cannot understand our language? How can they participate with us in worship if they have no context from their lives to associate with the language we use in our worship?

"Saved by the Lamb" is another expression that might have been significant in an agrarian culture where shepherds and flocks were common, where sacrificing an unblemished lamb carried the weight of social and political tradition. But what does it mean in a world where technology connects us, where "without blemish" does not conjure up images of a spotless lamb. Where even the idea of being "saved" rarely comes with spiritual connotations? We need to translate our faith and our risen Savior into this time and place by using language that is not jargon but real in the time and place where we live! In the end, we dishonor our Lord by mouthing expressions that we ourselves can hardly understand or relate to.

Lest you think I think we should abandon the ideas and themes behind many of these expressions, I do not think so. ...No ...there is a role for parents and the church in partnership to teach our children these great truths of the faith, which include explaining these expressions and concepts. They are deeply rooted in our faith tradition and history and in revelation as well. The church needs resources that make this "translation" a priority. To date I have not seen such efforts in the community of faith.

Another language that separates us from others in a social context is the language of academia. The words and thoughts of the great thinkers can divide us BUT can also draw us into their world. What allows us to enter to their thoughts. To enter their ideas is not so much their use of language but our ability to understand it, our exposure to it, and ultimately our involvement in the ideas that their words express. Spend a little time on any university campus and you will hear students complain about the difficulty of reading the latest essay assigned in Sociology: "Why can't that guy write in English?" A pride exist among academics that their language is somehow above the rest of us. Arguably there is probably a place for much of the erudite language that fills academic journals, but is that true in the church? Shouldn't the church be a place where the humblest and lowest among us can come and find a place?

The third area where I believe that we exclude others from our worship is in our use of ritualized or "formal" language. Many of our great hymns are packed with ritualized language that has no place in the common tongue of today. While King James English is beautiful, we need to remember that at the time of the writing of this translation, this "English" was the language of the common man. Shakespeare's language itself was the language of the masses. It may sound "high" and "grand" to us but that is simply because we do not speak that way. And the differences separate it from our normal conversation; this separation almost gives the language a superior aspect. And our use of it in formal settings elevates it again. So, we use "thee" and "thou" and "giveth" as if by doing so we are giving God more respect than if we used "you" and "gives." An argument could be made for using "thee" to acknowledge God's supremacy over us, but that we slide in and out of this language without any rhyme or reason, making its use confusing at best and alienating to outsiders at worst. And we sing hymns that use these kinds of words because that is the language they were written in. In the end though, these formal words do not provide a consistent posture of honor and respect for God. Our communities do not worship with a shared understanding that "thee" is how we address the Creator of the universe. My experience is that we are just a little schizophrenic when it comes to our language of worship. We use "thee" and "you" and various other formal and informal addresses with no consistent context or pattern. And more troubling to me is we do not engage any other person in our lives in such a confusing manner. Why is our God then subject to such confusing and inconsistent patterns of communication?

These expressions separate our children and outsiders from our worship because they are the language of some other time and some other people. When I taught high school students in California, I was aware of how important it was that the words I used communicated clearly and effectively to them. I knew their connection to me was dependent to a degree on their sense that I spoke their language (at least to a degree). How much more important is it in our churches we communicate the deep things of faith in ways that communicate to one another, our children and those who may be seeking God in our midst?

Now consider the question, "What language is most appropriate for worship?" This is the most difficult question. How does a university community whose congregation is filled with professors, students and others who share a deep love of learning answer? Probably, different from a rural community whose focus is on the weather and the crops and the needs of those less fortunate in the community. But I believe that there are several shared principles that apply:

- We must avoid jargon of all kinds: religious, secular, age-based, all of it. Our words of prayer and worship must take the truths of our faith and bring them to life in the context where the community of Christ lives. We must translate the truth of Christ—redemption, sin, sacrifice—all of it into concepts that meet modern men and women where they live. That will never mean abandoning the history of God's work among His people beginning with Adam nor will it mean ignoring the deep symbols embedded in the Jewish experience of Yahweh. But it will mean that we must always and everywhere seek to translate those truths into the lives of people today by using language that our children and outsiders can understand and hopefully connect with.

- We must balance the depth of our faith with its simplicity. It is profound beyond any understanding and yet it is also simple. "I tell you the truth, unless you change and become like little children, you will never enter the kingdom of God" (Mt. 18:3). Our language must recognize that tension and seek to build bridges of understanding.

- And finally, we must, I believe, purge our prayers and hymns of language that belong in the 18th or 19th centuries. The great hymns of yesterday speak of the truths of our faith; it is a disservice to their writers when we insist on keeping words that reflect an archaic language. I am confident that those men and women who penned those words will rejoice that the truth they wrote of is still sung today by young and old with gusto. I remember a time in a small group at our home when I tried to get the group to sing "How Great Thou Art" in modern English. It was difficult for some to replace the "thou" with "you" and "art" with "are" because of tradition. One member said, "I cannot sing it any other way; that is the way I learned it and I love it that way." While such sentimentality is understandable, I do not believe it advances the cause of the

8: CULTURE MATTERS

Kingdom. Sentimental attachment to words that do not communicate to others the truths of our faith does not seem consistent with a missionary church called to bring others into a saving relationship with Jesus. Young people today are turned off by songs with words that scream of a world that is long gone. Many of us used to think that our own parents were out of touch because of the language that characterized their interactions. All we must do to see the absurdity of some of the church's behavior in this area is to watch a television show from the sixties. Few of us would say "groovy" to positively describe a party because the word no longer fits in our cultural context. The church's language is no different. Why not sing the song in Latin? If tradition is to govern how we worship, then the logical consequence is that we should return to the rituals and language of the past. When we come together to worship, we come as a community to respond to God collectively. We come needing to uphold the human and divine bridges that join us to Him and to one another. Language is a critical element of such bridges.

In addition to language, remembrance is important in our worship. Experiencing worship in American churches, I see systematic attempts to ensure remembrance is part of Sunday worship. For example, times of confession, hymns that remind us of God's mighty hands at work, liturgical prayers or statements that affirm our journey of faith. In so far as these things seek to cause us to remember, they can be powerful. My struggle with the implementation of these things is that often the focus in them is not on God Himself but on our feelings and us. Take the church's use of hymns for example. Many of the greatest and most beloved hymns of church history are a regular element of worship in many churches. My concern is that many hymns are directed at the audience in the church. They are what I have come to call "campfire songs." They are suitable around a campfire where we remind ourselves of what we believe or retelling the stories that have impacted us on our individual faith journey. Their audience is the group around the fire, not our living God. They speak of Him but are not speaking to him!

One of my favorite hymns is a perfect example: "To God Be the Glory." If we look at the verses, we find they are written in the third person: "To God be the glory great things **He has done** and great our rejoicing through Jesus **His son**." A powerful melody and rhythm and words that remind us of what we hold to be true, but this hymn is not a hymn of worship on a couple of counts:

- It is not directed to God
- It announces truths of the faith but does not praise the author of our faith
- Though it confesses the truth we hold dear, it does not confess OUR need to OUR Creator

But the hymn does celebrate our faith and remind us of the God we worship and serve. See how I said that: "it reminds us of the God we worship and serve." The hymn by itself is not an act of worship; worship is our response to the truths enumerated in the song. If this song is used as a prelude to "acts of worship" in a congregation, then it might occupy an important place in an order of worship. The problem as I see it is that songs like this one appear sandwiched among other songs directed to God as songs of praise, adoration or confession.

Let's look at another of my favorite hymns: "All Hail the Power of Jesus' Name." Again, we find that this powerful and beautiful hymn is written in the third person: "Bring forth the royal diadem and

8: CULTURE MATTERS

crown ***Him Lord of all.***" It announces the appropriate behavior from those who would worship the Lord of all. The first verse proclaims, "Let angels prostrate fall." An act of worship by us might just be falling prostrate together before God on Sunday morning. Can't you just see individualistic American evangelicals down on their faces as orthodox Jews do before the Wailing Wall or in the presence of the Torah? This hymn is wonderful and can be an aid in worship, but it is not an act of worship. In fact, I believe that much of what we do as congregations in our worship services may not be worship at all, not meeting the elements of worship presented by Scripture so far.

John Hankerson

IX

Elements of Worship

When He made man, His purpose was man should love and honor Him. To praise Him for the wonderfully ordered complexity and variety of His world, using it according to His will, and so enjoying both it and Him. And though man has fallen, God has not abandoned His first purpose. Still, He plans that a great host of mankind should come to love and honor Him. His ultimate objective is to bring them to a state in which they <u>please Him entirely and praise Him adequately</u>. A state in which He is all in all to them. Where He and they rejoice continually in the knowledge of each other's love. <u>Men rejoicing in the saving love of God</u>, set upon them from all eternity, and God rejoicing in the responsive love of men, drawn out of them by grace through the gospel. (J.I. Packer, Knowing God)

Often after Sunday morning I will ask those who have been in church with me what they thought of the service. Responses vary depending, I suspect, on what exactly each person came expecting to find that morning. Some are so excited about the message or the delivery style of the message that all they can talk about is what a terrific job Pastor did in his sermon. Others find great satisfaction in the music used on that occasion. Still others will comment: "I didn't get anything out of it." A friend of mine recently got a comment like this one and responded, "That's O.K. because it wasn't for you." When he told me what he had said, I was struck by the deep insight represented by his response. Sunday morning worship is not for us; it is for God. Don't get me wrong! I find no evidence to suggest in

Scripture that we shouldn't get something out of worship, but Scripture does not teach that worship is for man. Unlike the Sabbath, which Jesus makes clear, is "for man," worship is at its heart totally for God. It is our response to Him and though I am confident that we are blessed through it, our blessing is irrelevant in how we should plan and carry out worship in our churches today.

If we were to direct our worship to God, what might that look like and what elements would it include? I believe that worship begins with:

- Sharing a common understanding of why we gather on Sunday mornings (Pastors need to teach their congregations the "rules of the game" so real community can happen.)
- Focusing on Him
    - In our music
    - In our prayers
    - In our actions
- Ensuring the church understands the elements of worship and the order. This means if we sing songs about God, the congregation knows these songs are there for us to collectively affirm and remember what He has done and then respond to His work in our lives.
- Lessening the "performance aspect" that often emerges in leading worship
- Ensuring the language we use, and the actions of worship speak into the culture and times of the congregation

The elements of our worship have already appeared throughout the texts of Scripture, but I would like to look at one text that perhaps captures the heart of worship. It is in Paul's second letter to the

9: ELEMENTS OF WORSHIP

Church at Corinth. Almost immediately he identifies one obvious element of worship, namely our praise. He writes, "Grace and peace to you from God our father and the Lord Jesus Christ. Praise be to the God and Father of our Lord Jesus Christ" (1:2-3). He is reminding the church of two things: God is "our father" and the father of Jesus. He is worthy of praise because, unspoken here, Jesus the son has saved us from death. He also reminds them that God is their father as well making them brothers of Jesus. Praise belongs in our worship!

The second element of worship that appears in this text is thanksgiving. Paul writes, "But thanks be to God, who always leads us in triumphal procession in Christ and through us spreads everywhere the fragrance of the knowledge of him." He is thankful for God's work through him among the gentiles, for God's work in the church at Corinth, and for the fact that he can trust his Father in everything.

The third element of worship that appears in this text is humility. As Paul describes his attempts to visit the church and share life with them without burdening them, he makes several profound statements about his understanding of his place before his Father. In sharing about the hardship he experienced before writing the letter he writes:

We were under great pressure, far beyond our ability to endure, so we despaired even of life. Indeed, in our hearts we felt the sentence of death. But this happened that we might not rely on ourselves but on God, who raises the dead. (1:8-9)

Paul is keenly aware that his very life is in the hands of God and the work he is doing depends completely on God's involvement. He reminds us that we must live lives that "rely not on ourselves but on God." He brings this point home again when he writes:

> *Not that we are competent to claim anything for ourselves, but our competence comes from God. He has MADE us competent as ministers of a new covenant—not of the letter but of the spirit; for the letter kills, but the Spirit gives life. (3:5-6)*

Perhaps my favorite in this string of reminders of our status as beloved creatures of the heavenly king is this passage:

> *But we have this treasure in jars of clay to show that this all-surpassing power is from God and not from us. We are hard-pressed on every side but not crushed; perplexed but not in despair; struck down but not destroyed. We always carry around in our body the death of Jesus so the life of Jesus may be revealed in our body. (4:7-10).*

And what is the "body" he refers to above? In this passage Paul uses "we" prolifically because he is talking about the church, the "body of Christ." It is both our individual bodies that carry life and death but also the body of the church which shows to the world what it means to die in Christ and to be made alive. How better it is for the world to see this lived out than to see believers living in humility. Making them aware of their own frailties and weaknesses and sin and rejoicing in the rescue that our faith affords us? Worship must fundamentally portray our humble and contrite spirit before the God who has saved us! In addition to humility, our worship must include our confession, for how else do we proclaim our need for a Savior? How else do we acknowledge our brokenness? How else do we stand together as sinners who have been forgiven and restored into a relationship with the Father? How else do we NOT follow Moses' example and hide our face from those around us, afraid if they see we are normal, mortal, frail and broken, we or maybe even God will be embarrassed. Consider the song I previously mentioned, "Give me the strength to be weak so others can see you are working in me." It proclaims we need to be real people to the world around us; the church needs to be real so Christ can be proclaimed.

I am reminded of growing up Catholic where confession is one of the first actions that are part of the mass (confession is also a significant element of an individual's life in the church). As an altar boy, I learned the "Confiteor Deo" in Latin and thought little of it at the time. But now I see that the liturgy recognized the importance of corporate confession, something I fear that the Protestant and evangelical world has diminished the importance of over time.

Maybe worship is as simple as that: confession, thanksgiving, and praise/adoration. Perhaps everything else acts in service to these three elements.

John Hankerson

X

The Order of Worship

To worship is to quicken the conscience by the holiness of God. It is to feed the mind with the truth of God. And to purge the imaginations by the beauty of God, to open the heart to the love of God, to devote the will to the purpose of God. (William Temple)

Richard Foster writes, "Worship is our response to the overtures of love from the heart of the Father. It is kindled within us only when the Spirit of God touches our human spirit." That spirit-to-Spirit connection is what we seek to enable in our worship. I humbly offer the following as **potential** (not necessarily prescriptive) ingredients of our worship that in some combination can facilitate this spirit-to-Spirit connection individually and among the body when we gather:

- Confession
- Celebration
- Corporate prayer
- Individual prayer with the body
- Testimonies
- Drama
- Children's events
- Scripture reading
- Responsive reading

- Teaching
- Sharing of praise and needs with the body

The challenge before us is to examine these "ingredients" against what we have learned from Scripture about worship: its music, language, nature, and focus. Then we can build an order of worship that fits our culture, community and time. And within that order, vary the things we do. For example: a drama to declare the glory of God, a children's story to remind us of what He has done for us, etc. ensure that our focus is always on Him, and let our language and music reflect both the local body and the Church of God throughout history. I was reminded our concept of worship is narrow when a **pastor said after singing**, "It is so good that we have spent this time in worship together." The implication was clear that it is primarily through song/music that we experience and do worship. It is my experience in several churches recently that the music portion of the service is essentially what worship leaders refer to as "worship. I believe it is much more. It can give us a taste of the divine kingdom here on earth; and that it can more fully express what it means for us to "bow down" before our God and Creator.

Below is a simple outline that focuses on six elements of worship that I offer as essential to our community practice. I will leave the specific content open-ended to be chosen to fit the culture and community of faith that has gathered to worship.

- *Greetings, Welcome and Announcements*
  (The family has gathered and there are things the family needs to know)
    - *Greet the family, especially newcomers*
    - *Share important announcements about our life together*
    - *Share the purpose of our time: i.e. what is worship?*

10: THE OEDER OF WORSHIP

- Open our time of worship with prayer

- Call to Worship
  These are just a few of the ways to call the body into worship:
  - Scripture Reading
  - Dramatic event
  - Song(s)

- Declaration of our God's Goodness, His Mighty Deeds, His Saving Grace

  There are so many ways that we can declare our God's goodness:
  - I think of many of the great hymns of the church: *Oh, The Deep Love of Jesus, All Hail the Power of Jesus' Name, To God be the Glory.* All these proclaim in song the greatness of God. This is why I do not consider them to be praise or adoration: they are not sung to God but to announce what we believe and share together as members of His family.
  - Congregational sharing of what God has done in individual lives over the past week or years
  - Recitation of the Apostles Creed or reading a Psalm together
  - Corporate prayers of thanksgiving
  - Songs of celebration

- Acknowledgment of our Need

  Scripture reading reminding us of our need and sin
    - Corporate prayers of confession (responsive reading, recitation of a confession, individual prayers acknowledging our sin and need
    - Silent, individual prayers of confession
    - Songs
    - Drama
    - Corporate prayers of petition

- Teaching from God's Word
  I wrestled with where to place this element. It often comes at the end of a service, but I am not convinced that is where teaching or a sermon belongs. When we are presented with God's Word, it requires a response from us, which is why I included a time of praise and offering <u>afterwards</u> in this order. These two elements are significant and should not become an afterthought. This element could easily be placed after the *Call to Worship* above.

- *Praise for His Goodness* (I imagine an extended time of praise and offering)
    - Songs of praise directed towards God
    - Scripture that declares our praise
    - Individual prayers of praise among the congregation

- Offering and Benediction

It seems simple: we greet and welcome the family together, we are called to worship, we pronounce the greatness of our God (bow down). We recognize our need (bow down), we hear His word to us, we praise Him for his goodness, we give to His work among us, and we are sent out with His blessing.

John Hankerson

Afterword

Studying the nature of worship as presented in Scripture and wrestling with my own feelings has been a deep joy for me. It reminds me of what God has done for me personally and of the promise of what His Life in us means for our community life together.

It took me back in time to two formative events in my Christian life. The first was my time at Peninsula Bible Church in Palo Alto where Ray Steadman taught. When one weekly Sunday evening service called Body Life gave me a glimpse into what a church body could be. While it was not billed as a worship service, worship did indeed happen there. There were a few songs, a brief reflection from Scripture and then an extended time of sharing and prayer together as a body. Individuals would share praises or needs and then the larger group gathered there would pray for that individual or offer affirmations of their praises. Many would pray out loud from their seats and after a time, a pastors would close the time. Then another individual would share, and the process would repeat. We were a body gathered to pray for and support one another and to hear of the wonderful deeds of our God in the lives of our neighbors. And this was a group that usually numbered 800 or more; the church was usually filled. I saw vulnerability and need (bowing down) and the powerful work of prayer in lives around me. Worship happened there!

The second event (an experience) was a group of schoolboys (young men) who had agreed to be part of a "Discipleship Group" that I led through a local Presbyterian church. We met every week for nearly three years to study the Bible and fellowship. Most of the guys were sophomores, though over the three years one or two dropped out and one or two joined. What was most profound for me was the experience I had as we studied and worshipped together. Can you imagine a group of high school guys singing songs of praise together, holding hands as we prayed for one another, and sharing hurts and needs with one another?

We were a "body" that loved the Lord, loved one another, prayed for one another, and bore one another's struggles. Our singing was often off-key, but our hearts knew only one thing: that our God was with us and in us and working to transform each of us into the likeness of His Son. (A special "thank you" to Don who led us with his guitar and his warm, loving and vulnerable self, who taught us in his humility what brotherly love looked like. In that setting with those young men, I experienced a glimpse of heaven, of what worship can be.

I believe that these experiences marked my soul with a taste of Heaven and eternity. And I am so grateful to these young men who shared their lives with me as well as their journey of faith. Thank you Don Barrie, Van Schalin, Steve Holloway, Tom Bryce, Shawn Ritchey, Tom Hethorn, Joe Fisch, Bill McDonald, and Chuck Durous. You have shown me what our life and fellowship in Christ can be!

In a Bible the group gave to me, one of them wrote: "That first night that I left, I cried; the second night I sang. This body of Christ amazes me. In them was/is life." This note still brings tears to my eyes, tears of gratefulness to our God and to these fellow travelers on this journey of faith. The young man who wrote these words has passed from Pancreatic cancer, but his memorial celebration was

AFTERWORD

profound. A witness to God's intimate activity in his life and in the life of his wife and five children. And in the lives of all who spoke of their husband/father with deep love and appreciation and gratitude for his life of faith which touched each of them. And the church was filled with others whom he touched with his deep faith. I was privileged to have shared time with him in this group.

Having been an English teacher for a time in my career, I have come to realize that words and details matter to me (just imagine the "red" correction marks on essays I graded). My students will testify that I was a stickler for words and details. Thinking about the ideas presented here, I realize there are details that I hope were clear. Hoping they might make a positive difference for believers in their individual time of worship and for the Church in its corporate expression of worship. Let me close with a few of these details:

- Language matters.
  The words we use can draw others into our community or push them away (think of our youth relating to "thee" and "thou" or the non-believer understanding sin, redemption, salvation, the blood of the lamb)

- Songs are not necessarily "worship."
  Some of our music declares truths about our God while other music is an expression of our praise or thanksgiving TO our God

- Worship is essentially our bowing down before our God. Confession, acknowledgment of our NEED, declaration of His greatness

- Worship is admitting our utter dependence on Him.

"That we are not sufficient in ourselves to claim anything as coming from us. Our sufficiency is from God, who has made us ministers of a new covenant, not of the letter but of the Spirit. For the letter kills, but the Spirit gives life." (II Cor. 3:5-6 RSV)

- Culture matters.
  Worship should reflect the community of believers consistent with the truths of Scripture

My prayer is simple. I pray something here will enable individual worship and prayer to open the presence of God here and now. I pray each of us is drawn closer into His embrace and these individual experiences of a renewed worship will transform our life together and our life with Him.

John Hankerson is available for interviews, For more information send inquiries to: info@advbooks.com

we bring dreams to life ™
www.advbookstore.com

www.ingramcontent.com/pod-product-compliance
Lightning Source LLC
LaVergne TN
LVHW051505070426
835507LV00022B/2932